Get Stitched

Learn to Knit with **Tom Daley**

Get Stitched

Learn to Knit with Tom Daley

Get Stitched with **15** Simple and Stylish **Knitting Patterns**

Popular Designs from the Made With Love Collection

PHOTOGRAPHY BY DANIEL FRASER

Contents

06 Introduction

14 How to Use This Book

18 Yarn Essentials

26 Knitting Essentials

84 Knitted Accessories

  86 Ribbed Dickie
  92 Leg Warmers
  96 Balaclava
 102 Odd Socks
 108 Long Scarf

TOM DALEY

112

Knitted Garments

114   Fringe Sweater

120   Cable Sweater

126   Top Down Fairisle Sweater

132   Varsity Cardigan

142   Swirl Vest

150   Balloon Sleeve Cardigan

156   Hooded Poncho

164

Knitted Homewares

164   Patchwork Blanket

174   Dog Hat

178   Stroller Blanket

182

Caring For Your Makes

GET STITCHED

Introduction →

Without knitting I may not have won a gold medal at the Tokyo Olympics. Now, I'm not saying that I couldn't have done it. I'd been diving for 20 years and Tokyo was my fourth Olympics. Essentially, I'd been training my whole life to win Olympic gold. I'd put in an enormous amount of effort and made many sacrifices; it wasn't an easy journey, nor one without preparation. However, it was the calmness and focus that knitting provided me when sitting up in the spectator stands between events, that helped to stop my mind spiralling into anxious thoughts and stay present in the moment, aided by the rhythmic motion of creating the stitches with my hands.

Team Great Knittin'

When the photographs of me knitting poolside at the Olympics went viral, it felt quite surreal because I was just sitting there doing what I love to do, not thinking about anything or anyone else. I now wonder whether knitting may have been my secret weapon in that competition. Due to the COVID-19 pandemic, there were no spectators at the event and our families were at home on the other side of the world, so for me, knitting gave me a concentration and a way to pass the time without getting stressed. I loved the fact that, after seeing me knit, other people thought about taking up knitting too and I was happy to be flying the flag for Team Great Knittin'!

When people talk to me about knitting – if they don't already knit themselves (when they do they will usually get out their latest project to show me!) – they often say 'I would love to do that, but it looks so complicated.' I promise you do not need to be a crafting genius or have exceptional dexterity to have a go at knitting. It's simply a series of interconnected loops that are formed by a continuous length of yarn (that's just another term for wool, or cotton, or whichever fibre you choose!) using needles to create a pattern. With a bit of patience and concentration, anyone can do it.

When I first started knitting, what I found to be the hardest part was holding the needles and yarn at the same time as trying to make the stitches – I dropped loads along the way. My knitting looked atrocious, but I persevered and, as my technique improved, I fell in love with the simple joy of the craft. Now I knit in every spare moment I have. It has brought me so much pleasure and allows me to be mindful and focus on the task at hand. If you are focusing on knitting, counting stitches, and creating textures, there's no space for other thoughts to creep in, and it allows me to reset, like meditation.

It's also an incredibly creative outlet; your knitting can be whatever you choose it to be, and it will always be unique to you. It allows me to step outside of mainstream fast fashion to make my own catwalk-inspired looks that are totally individual to me, and that I know I'm going to love and feel amazing wearing.

Knitting is about much more than just making something new to wear or to gift to a loved one. Every item I have knitted tells a story; from the sweater that I made during the lockdown in 2020 (I was so proud of making something I could actually wear!) to the Olympic cardigan I finished while competing at the games in Tokyo, my projects are filled with colourful memories of the times they were created, literally knitted into every stitch. At Paris

2024, my fifth Olympics, where I won a silver medal, I worked on another design themed around the event. A sweater in red, white and blue – the colours of not only the Union Flag of the UK but also the Tricolore of France – with PARIS 24 emblazoned on the front, with the A in the form of the iconic Eiffel Tower, and my name DALEY knitted in intarsia across the back. I love how my knitting has become synonymous with the Olympics. As someone wrote on X, 'The Olympics only officially starts when Tom Daley gets his knitting out!'

How I started

I first picked up a pair of knitting needles after my husband Lance suggested that it might be a good way of relaxing at the poolside during diving training and competitions. During the bigger competitions, there can be a lot of waiting around and, for me, this was when the worries started to take hold. Lance told me that a lot of actors knit during downtime on a film set as a way of taking their minds away from their work. I decided to have a go. At the start of 2020, I watched a YouTube video and then practised on the plane during a long flight to a competition in Canada. I attempted to knit a simple square, but I ended up with a scrap of fabric riddled with holes. It was a disaster! While I was in Montreal, two of the other springboard divers – one from Australia and the other from Russia – spotted my attempts and both helped me to get started properly. They sat alongside me and taught me the basics and my second effort looked much better. This taught me another lesson about knitting, it's universal and can create a natural trust and ease between crafters.

By the end of that trip, I had made a scarf and I haven't looked back since! The year 2020 was a time when many of us were isolating at home – working or trying to keep busy – and with pools and training gyms closed, it gave me both the time and opportunity to practise my craft. As an athlete, I'm continuously trying to develop and hone my skills. While it would be great to make lots of scarves to wear myself or gift to others, I realised that I wouldn't be progressing with the craft if that was all I made. So, with each item I knitted, I tried to learn a new technique or stitch. In doing this, I became more confident in my ability.

Through knitting, I found a new challenge, something separate and different to my diving, that allowed me to both switch off from existing worries, and also to keep my brain engaged on an activity. I found that once you begin to understand the mechanics of the stitches, you can make them work for you, find ways to correct mistakes and discover the determination to follow your projects through to the end. Hopefully, resulting in a cool new item of clothing or eye-catching accessory to show off. Not to mention a great sense of achievement and pride.

Since then, I have created hundreds of items for my friends and family, I have launched my own Made with Love clothing brand, and I have designed and knitted the scarves for my friend, designer Daniel Fletcher's A/W22 London Fashion Week show, and designed and made a bolero-style cardigan for Gillian Anderson to wear in the Netflix show *Sex Education*, which we then auctioned off for charity. I have also become a part of a really welcoming community of knitters. It's such a sociable activity and everyone is so encouraging about each other's creations. It's like a safe space of totally different, but like-minded individuals all sharing brilliant colours, amazing designs, and exciting textures. It's a world I knew nothing about until I became a part of it. Now I never want to leave and I want to invite everyone I know to the party!

" **Learning to *knit* is is a *gift* for life.**

TOM DALEY
"

Love

Made with...

Made with love for those you love

There's nothing quite like receiving a handmade gift. Knowing that the maker has poured their thought, creativity, talent and time into tailoring a gift just for you, well, simply grabbing something at the shops or clicking "add to basket" just cannot compare. With a handmade gift, you know that the person who made it has really invested love in each stitch. Creating a handmade gift takes time and effort, which cannot be exchanged or imitated, so the recipient will find it all the more precious. Plus it will be the only gift like it on the entire planet – it doesn't get more personal than that!

I love the fact that I can create something unique for someone, tailor made to suit their style and tastes and completely personalised to them. All of the projects in this book are designed to be recipes that you can adapt and customise to suit you or the person you are making it for, that's the beauty of making something by hand rather than buying "off the shelf". One of the first items I made was a scarf for my mum for Mother's Day and I was able to choose a purple yarn, which is her favourite colour. I have always found seeing the reactions of my friends and family when I gift them something that I have made really special and that's all part of the fun for me.

In *Get Stitched*, I have included the patterns for some of my favourite items for gifting, from a mohair scarf that can be knitted to any length, a knitted dog hat for that beloved pooch to a stroller blanket for a newborn, I hope these thoughtful gifts will surprise and delight the recipient.

How I approach design

I love the process of choosing yarns, colours, stitch textures and shapes when making items for my favourite people. From picking out the softest and warmest fibres, to deciding on acid brights or soft pastel colours, it is so individual. I draw inspiration from so many places; from watching reels on Instagram to flicking through editorial fashion shoots in magazines, from couture collections on the runway to the street style I see every day outside my front door in London.

I love using vivid colours for my makes. Sometimes I find that when you're buying ready-to-wear from a store, the rationale is to buy black or grey or another muted colour that goes with everything. Or you're limited to those colours that the fashion brands have decided that everyone must wear that season. But if you're choosing to make something from scratch, you have the choice to put any colours you like into it. Plus with knitting, you can choose the fibre from which the fabric will be made too!

For each project in this book, I have given the yarn and shade that I have used, but you can make it any colour or yarn you want – just make sure to work a tension swatch (see page 74) before you dive into the project if you are substituting the yarn. I have included some of my favourite contemporary pastels and popping neons alongside classic and dramatic monochromes. But if you want to substitute the colour for all black or bright pink and lime green? Go for it! Show your personality through what you make.

Once you have an understanding of how the different knitting stitches and techniques work and how to use them to create fabrics and shapes, you can get creative and experiment. One of the greatest things about knitting is that it really doesn't matter too much if something goes wrong. I have made many things in the past, where the sleeves didn't quite fit or the sizing came up a bit off. I even once made a sweater that I couldn't get over my head! If this happens, don't panic! You can simply unravel your work and start again. It's just another opportunity to practice your craft and improve your skills. My advice is always just to enjoy the process, even if it doesn't go right every time – it's all part of the knitting journey!

How to Use This Book

No matter what your experience –
whether you have yet to pick up a
pair of knitting needles or you are
a seasoned pro – I hope this book
inspires you to take up a new craft
and set aside some time for yourself.
I have used some my favourite yarns
and knitting stitches to make fun,
original and vibrant designs for
unique handknits – I really hope you
love them as much as I do!

In this section, I guide you through all the basics, from casting on your first stitches through to fastening off, weaving in your yarn ends and sewing up a project. Then I share my favourite designs for creating quick-to-make accessories and simple homewares up to more complex garments, some with stitch textures, some with colourwork and some with both!

I also demystify the cryptic code of knitting, which can sometimes read like a foreign language! Once you get started and become familiar with a few key terms, it's not as complex as it looks – I promise! I do think it's a bit like learning an unfamiliar language or taking up a new sport – it just takes a bit of practice to become proficient.

Have you ever heard of the concept of muscle memory? The more you repeat a movement, the easier you find it and soon it becomes second nature. Before long, you'll be able to knit while chatting or watching a boxset. Give it a week or two and your needles will be clacking away!

The speed at which you decide to work through the projects in this book is entirely up to you. If you're a more experienced knitter, you may wish to dip in and out of the designs that most catch your eye, but if you're a beginner, starting by checking the skill level assigned to each project.

Take as long as you need to hone each new skill and refer back to the 'how to' guides; while chunky knitted fabric can be quick to grow, the beauty of knitting is that it's a slow craft – a moment to unwind and get lost in your making – and that's all part of the enjoyment. If you drop a stitch or make a hole, don't stress! It's never a disaster. You can always pick up a dropped stitch or unravel a few rows and re-knit them.

Got pressing things to do that are not knitting-related? Although it will become hard to imagine what could be more important – don't worry about that either. You can always put the needles down once you've worked a few rows and pick it up again as soon as you have a spare moment. Just be sure to keep your WIP (work in progress) safely away from pets, children and nosy housemates. Most of all, just enjoy the process and the endless possibilities of what you can create.

Happy making!

Sizing

All the garments in this book are designed to be unisex and inclusive for all. Many people think that unisex items lean more towards boxy men's shapes that women can also wear. I like to think of it almost in reverse – flattering shapes that anyone can wear. Ultimately, you should always wear whatever makes you feel good.

Choosing a garment size

Sometimes it can be tricky to know the right garment size to knit from a pattern. Don't just plump for your usual clothing size as that may not match the dimensions that the pattern designer has used – every garment is designed to have a certain amount of ease, which differs from project to project. Ordinarily, garments are listed in generic sizes, such as small, medium, large and so on, but they will also include key measurements, such as the chest measurement. Children's garments are more usually presented as an age range, from 4 to 5 years, for example.

If you're unsure what size to choose, my advice is this: for comparison, take the measurements of your favourite sweater, cardigan or other garment that is similar in shape and fabric weight to the one you plan to make. This garment can be as tight-fitting or as loose-fitting as you wish, but bear in mind the amount of ease that has been designed into the garment you plan to make. Lie your existing garment flat and measure the chest width. Now find the closest match to that width on the size chart – that's the best size for you and the one that you're going to highlight to follow.

Following the pattern instructions

Pattern instructions will be written in more than one size. The smallest will be first and sit just outside the parentheses and then the larger sizes will follow inside the parentheses. When there is only one figure given in the instructions, this will apply to all sizes. When there is a 0 listed, then no stitches or rows are worked for that specific size. Remember this: if your size is the second in the size chart, it will always be the second in any sequence.

To ensure you always work the correct size when following lengthy pattern instructions, I advise highlighting or underlining the figures that correspond with your size in the pattern. This includes the number of balls of yarn you'll need to complete your project, the number of stitches to be cast on in the first row, the number of stitches or rows worked in a certain stitch pattern or colour, the number of times to repeat an instruction or the length of any section in centimetres or inches. Marking your specific size within the instructions simplifies reading the pattern as you work – your eyes can flick straight to the correct number. If your pattern is in a book like this one, you may prefer to photocopy the relevant page.

Checking your tension

Before you start any new project, always check your tension or gauge (see page 66). If your tension varies from that given in the pattern by even one stitch or row, change your knitting needle size up or down accordingly otherwise your garment will end up a different size from the dimensions stated on the size chart. Over a larger piece, any difference in tension or gauge will be further exaggerated.

Yarn Essentials

There are many different types of yarns available in a multitude of fibres, colours, and textures. Yarn is one of my favourite things; I am like a kid in a candy store when choosing yarn! When selecting the yarn for any project, the two most important factors are fibre and weight.

A quick guide

Fibre

Anything can be used as a yarn – as long as it is a continuous length that can be knitted; it can be done. Yarns are broadly split into different categories.

1 • Animal fibres

Sheep's wool, alpaca, mohair, and silk are all examples of animal fibres. Wool is a firm favourite with knitters. Spun from the fleece of a sheep, it's durable and a great insulator so will keep you at the right temperature. It can also absorb moisture without feeling wet. Great for bobble hats in rainy weather! It can feel a bit scratchy against the skin, but different sheep breeds produce wool with various qualities. Merino wool is spun from the fleece of that breed of sheep and is softer than regular wool.

2 • Plant fibres

Cotton, hemp, bamboo, and linen are examples of plant fibres. These are non-allergenic and cooling, so are ideal for warmer months. Cotton is my go-to yarn choice for summer knits.

3 • Synthetic fibres

Nylon, acrylic, and polyester are all synthetic fibres. These tend to be inexpensive, wash well, and are easy to care for. These yarns are particularly hard-wearing so are ideal for items that you might use every day like cushions and throws. Synthetics are sometimes blended with natural fibres to enhance washability and strength. The synthetic fibres can help bind yarns like wool together to stop shedding or shrinking.

Whilst synthetic yarns may not seem as appealing as animal or natural fibres, they are becoming the preferred choice of vegans. If you're looking for yarns made from non-animal fibre sources or are concerned about the consumption of water or other natural resources in the production of some yarns, then there is an increasing number of synthetic options available.

Weight

All these fibres are spun to create yarns that are made up of one or more plies – or strands – twisted together. Some yarns are more twisted than others so have a slightly different quality, but generally it gives a yarn strength, making it harder to break when working with it.

Two single strands twisted together make a 2-ply yarn, or if eight are used, this is an 8-ply. The thickness of the yarn is decided by the thickness of the individual plies, not the number of plies, so a 4-ply yarn is not necessarily thicker than a single ply, but the general rule is the lower the number of plies, the finer the yarn. I love bulky roving yarns – which are long and narrow fibres – as the projects work up so quickly. I just love the personality of these yarns!

While I prefer knitting with bulky yarns as your work grows so quickly, such a heavyweight yarn isn't suitable for every project. Each yarn is classified as a certain weight, which refers to the thickness of the overall yarn. They can be lace weight or superfine through to super bulky or jumbo. As a general rule, the weights of yarns fall within standardised categories assigned by the Craft Yarn Council in the U.S. to help knitters and crocheters choose the right thickness of yarn to ensure every project is a success (see page 22).

Yarn weight category and symbol	LACE	SUPER FINE	FINE	LIGHT	MEDIUM	BULKY	SUPER BULKY	JUMBO
Type of yarns in category	2-ply (fingering)	3-ply (sock), baby	4-ply (sport), baby	Double knitting (light worsted)	Aran (worsted), afghan	Chunky (bulky), craft, rug	Super chunky (super bulky)	Jumbo
Knit tension (gauge) in stocking (stockinette) stitch to 10cm (4 inches)	33–40 sts	27–32 sts	23–26 sts	21–24 sts	16–20 sts	12–15 sts	7–11 sts	6 sts and fewer
Recommended knitting needles in metric size	1.5–2.25mm	2.25–3.25mm	3.25–3.75mm	3.75–4.5mm	4.5–5.5mm	5.5–8mm	8–12.75mm	12.75mm and larger
Recommended knitting needles in U.S. size	000–1	1–3	3–5	5–7	7–9	9–11	11–17	17 and larger
Crochet tension (gauge) in double (single) crochet to 10cm (4 inches)	32–42 sts	21–32 sts	16–20 sts	12–17 sts	11–14 sts	8–11 sts	7–9 sts	6 sts and fewer
Recommended crochet hook in metric size	Steel hook 1.6–1.4mm	2.25–3.5mm	3.5–4.5mm	4.5–5.5mm	5.5–6.5mm	6.5–9mm	9–15mm	15mm and larger
Recommended crochet hook in U.S. size	Steel hook 6, 7, 8	B-1 to E-4	E-4 to 7	7 to I-9	1-9 to K-10½	K-10½ to M-13	M-13 to Q	Q and larger

Double-knitting or worsted is a medium-weight yarn and sits in the middle of the range. It's often used for hats, scarves, sweaters, and a myriad of other items because you can see the individual stitches. For beginners, I always suggest starting with a chunkier yarn, so bulky is my go-to choice. Once you have got to grips with the most comfortable way to hold the yarn and let it flow, your knitting will grow quite fast and that feels really rewarding.

Fibre choice is also important when starting out. Generally, I would recommend wool because it has a natural elasticity and is quite forgiving. A wool blend or super-wash wool is a good choice because as a blended synthetic fibre, it flows more easily. Cotton is also lovely to work with because it's strong and unlikely to break but is flat with less stretch and a bit slower to knit with. I would go for something mid-range – a decent quality but not too expensive!

As part of the instructions for every project in this book, you'll see the recommended weight of yarn to use. If you're shopping in store and don't know what you need – just ask. I would also consider the availability of what you need – the last thing you want to do is run out of yarn mid-project! In my opinion, it's best to buy a bit too much yarn so this doesn't happen and then use up any yarn remnants in smaller projects. Within the projects, there are a few smaller items that are ideal for smaller amounts of yarn.

Label talk

Yarn is packaged in different ways, but it will always be accompanied by a yarn label, which is sometimes called a ball band. The yarn is wound like a ball, skein, hank, or on a cone – basically in different shapes – with a helpful label, which you must always read carefully.

Shade names and dye lot numbers

Some brands label their yarns with a code for each different colour they offer. However, I prefer it when a yarn range has a name for each shade rather than a code number. Especially when the name is an evocative description of the shade of the yarn.

Knitters sometimes talk about dye lots, but what exactly does this mean? Well, yarns are available in many different natural and dyed colours. A dye lot is a batch of yarn that has been dyed at the same time, so even if yarns have the same shade name or code number, if they're dyed at different times, this means the colour could vary because of differences in temperature, dyeing time, and other factors. When you're buying yarn, make sure all the balls or skeins have been dyed in the same lot (they will have the same unique number) so the colour of the yarn is consistent throughout your project.

TOM'S TIP:

If you're giving a knitted item as a gift, include a yarn label (ball band) in the parcel so the recipient knows how to care for it and won't shrink it in the wash. If it's something for yourself or a family member, take a photo of the label so you can always refer back to the care instructions.

Reading yarn labels

Yarn labels are all slightly different and laid out in a variety of ways, but most packaging includes the following information:

The name of the **brand**.

The name of the **yarn**.

The **weight category** of the yarn (and if the yarn is from a U.S. manufacturer, also the relevant Craft Yarn Council symbol).

The **weight of the yarn** in grams or ounces that is packaged in the ball, skein, hank, or cone.

The **length of the yarn** in metres and/or yards.

The **fibre content**, including the percentages of each type of fibre that makes up the yarn.

The colour information, including the **shade name or number** and the **dye lot number**.

The **recommended knitting needle or crochet hook size** to achieve the given tension (gauge).

The **recommended tension (gauge)**, including number of stitches and rows to 10cm (4 in) (see page 66).

Care instructions, including washing, drying, and ironing – these instructions apply to the yarn as to any finished knitted or crocheted item.

Yarn Essentials

Substituting yarn

Yarn substitution is a term that describes using a different yarn to the one recommended in the pattern. With so many yarns available, understanding how to substitute one yarn for another is so useful. It gives you lots more choice when thinking about your next project and sourcing supplies. There are several reasons why you may want to substitute a yarn – maybe you're looking for a vegan-friendly alternative to animal fibres, or a yarn that's more affordable, or the recommended yarn is no longer available. You may even spot a yarn that you love and want to make something with it. It took me a while to feel confident with subbing yarns, but here are my tips for things to think about:

1 • Check the tension

The first step is to always check the tension (gauge). You will need to knit a decent-size swatch before continuing with your project. As well as ensuring your swatch gives the right tension (gauge), the designer will have ensured that the stitch pattern works with the yarn to create a certain effect. Solid-coloured and smooth yarns will give greater stitch definition than multi-coloured or tweedy yarns, for example. Even if something is 5mm (¼ inch) out, it may have a real impact on the size of the shape of the garment or the finished item.

2 • Think about fibre

When subbing yarns, look for alternatives with a similar fibre content, so they have a tension (gauge) close to the recommended yarn. Any slight difference between yarns may have a big knock-on effect on the way the stitches look. Generally, plant-based fibres don't have as much stretch as animal fibres, unless they're blended with elastane, acrylic, or polyester. The same garment designed in stretchy wool will look quite different when made up in flat cotton. A common substitution is a wool yarn for a wool blend yarn.

3 • Calculate the meterage

It's important to check meterage (yardage) – the length of the yarn within the ball, skein or hank – compared to the one you're substituting. This is so you don't run out of yarn, midway through your project. Every pattern will tell you how much yarn you need, so divide the amount specified in the pattern by the meterage (yardage) of the balls you want, to know what number to buy.

4 • Weigh everything up

While it's a good idea to stick with the recommended yarn weight, you can experiment by substituting two strands of light weight yarn for a single strand in a heavier weight. Remember to calculate the amount of yarn in metres or yards needed to complete the project. Doubling up yarns to create an interesting colour or textural effect is not always an exact science, so your tension (gauge) is the best guide.

Knitting Essentials

02

One of the greatest things about knitting is its simplicity. Because you only need a handful of items to get going, I find it to be the perfect hobby when I am travelling a lot for my diving. Chuck it all in a bag and off you go! If you are like me then you will have a couple of projects on the go at the same time. I always have a bigger one, like a sweater or blanket, that I knit at home and then something smaller and portable, like a scarf or hat, that I can take with me to work on when I am on the move.

Knitting kit list

As you turn the pages of this book, I share more of what I have learned about knitting. My initial advice is to start with just the basics and grow your knitting kit as you learn and progress. When you first start it is tempting to throw lots of money at beautiful needles and expensive yarn, but it makes more sense to buy items on a project-by-project basis and grow your knitting-essentials kit gradually.

As a bare minimum to start knitting, you need:

- Yarn
- Knitting needles
- Scissors
- Tape measure
- Yarn needle

You can buy these items almost anywhere including high-street stores, haberdashery sections of department stores, large hobby and craft retailers and online specialists. Increasingly, I like to support local spinners for quality small-batch yarns and independent retailers for knitting notions, which is the catch-all term for knitting needles and other tools and accessories.

- **Yarn**

In the beginning, yarns might all look the same to you but in terms of knitting, there are big differences. As you become more experienced, you will learn what types of yarn suit certain projects and how they can ensure everything you knit is a success.

- **Knitting needles**

Needles come in various shapes, sizes, and materials. The most common materials are metal, wood, bamboo, and plastic. There are several metal options including aluminium, stainless steel, brass, or nickel. The different sizes are based on needle diameter – the smaller the size, the thinner the width. These come in slightly different sizes, whether you are in the UK or the U.S.

To start with, I think larger straight needles are better for beginner knitters, so I would suggest trying bamboo needles because they are easy to work with, a bit less slippery, warm, and quite gentle on your hands. Some yarns, like cotton, can stick to bamboo making it harder if you are a beginner, but they can hold more silky yarns really easily. They are also strong and inexpensive. I also like the sound that they make; it is less metal on metal and more of a gentle tapping noise!

Some yarns will work better with certain materials and needle sizes, and generally heavier yarns are paired with larger-sized needles, whilst finer yarns are paired with thinner needles. Sharper points also make it easier to work with finer yarns, whilst rounder points are better for bulkier yarns and safer for kids. Check any pattern instructions for the suggested needle size. I would always say to experiment with material and length, as the more you knit, the more you will discover about how to create the type of knitted fabric you love.

Knitting Essentials

As well as straight needles, there are other styles:

Circular needles

These are two tapered needles connected by a flexible cord and are used to knit in a continuous round, for projects like hats, sweaters, and sleeves (see page 100). Like straight needles, circular needles are available in different sizes. With these, the weight of the work rests in your lap, so there is less strain on your hands, arms, and shoulders, so if you are making something big, like a blanket, I would always recommend using these. You are also less likely to drop a needle on the floor if you are knitting on the move. I love using circular needles.

Double-pointed needles

These needles (abbreviated to dpns) have a point at each end and come in packs of four or five. With these needles, stitches can be worked with one end and can be removed from the other end, avoiding the need to turn your work at the end of each row. They are used for knitting things in the round that are too small for circular needles, like socks. As a general rule, I prefer to use a circular needle with a smaller connecting wire rather than dpns for making smaller items, but this is down to individual preference.

Cable needles

These are very short needles with points at each end, and sometimes a bend in the middle, which are used to make a cable pattern (see page 125) by holding the stitches you are not actively using. Most people have two cable needles – one thin and one thick.

- ### Scissors

A small pair of scissors is an essential item, so you can snip as you go.

- ### Tape measure

This is necessary so that you can check your tension (gauge) square and measure the dimensions of your work. A wooden ruler can also be useful to check tension as, unlike a dressmaker's tape measure, it will not stretch and distort over time.

- ### Large-eyed yarn needle

You will use this needle to sew in any loose yarn ends and join your project pieces together (like joining together the front and back sides of a sweater). They come with large eyes so the yarn passes through them easily and are also slightly blunt at the tip so that they don't split the yarn. These needles come in packs where there will be a variety of sizes, just make sure the eye you of the needle you use is easily large enough to thread the yarn through.

- ### Other items

If you can see yourself getting the knitting bug, here are some other pieces you might like to collect. I found that I acquired them slowly as I gained more experience. They are not essential but useful to have!

Stitch holders

These hold open stitches when you are completing another part of your knitting or need your needles for another project. You can always improvise using safety pins, nappy pins, or even paper clips!

Knitting Essentials

Stitch markers
These are handy little tools that you can use to identify an important place in your knitting or keep track of increases and decreases. They come in different shapes and colours to fit your needles. If I am doing a project where I have to count lots of rows (like a 200-row project), every 10 rows I will clip on a safety pin-style stitch marker so I know where I am.

Row counters
Some stitch patterns are complicated, so row counters can help you keep track of which row you are on. With each row, you turn the wheel to the next number until you complete the required amount. You may prefer to write it down with a pen and paper (this is what I do).

Crochet hook
You will need a crochet needle for picking up dropped stitches in your knitting. Like knitting needles, crochet hooks are available in different sizes.

Dressmaking pins
These are used to hold pieces of knitting together before you sew them. Long, thick pins with large, coloured heads are easier to see and less likely to split the yarn.

Blocking board and blocking pins
Blocking helps to ensure that your knitting lies flat with lovely, neat edges. It is also a technique used to stretch and shape a piece of knitted fabric to the dimensions given in the pattern instructions. When you steam or spray block a knitted piece, you can manipulate it into the right shape and size. This also makes sewing up or finishing the garments easier. These boards come in a range of sizes and the pins will help you pin out the edges of your project. Blocking can also be done with a towel on a flat surface but having a board does make it easier.

Needle size gauge
This gadget shows you what size your knitting needles are. Simply poke them into the different size holes until you find the one that fits. This is useful for checking the size of vintage needles, which can be picked up cheaply in charity shops and thrift stores.

Bobbins
These are plastic frames that around which you can wrap different yarns. They are handy if you do a lot of colourwork because it means you don't have to work with full balls of each colour. Instead, you can wind off amounts of each one. I don't personally use them. I just have everything laid out on a table. Complex colourwork is not an on-the-go project!

Pompom maker
There are loads of ways to make pompoms. Clip-together pompom makers are really easy to use (see page 177), but sometimes I make them using two circles of cardboard or even by wrapping the yarn around my fingers.

Point protectors
These little rubber caps that cover the points of your knitting needles when you are not using them help to keep your stitches on your needles securely as your masterpiece progresses. This is a must-have if you are like me and always on the go or have small children who like to pick things up!

```
Of course, you can add
anything else you fancy to
  this kit list. You will find
  that craft shops, both online
   and on the high street, will
    be filled to the brim with
    tantalising tools and gadgets.
```

Knitting Essentials

Knitting basics →

Right. It's time to get knitting. Grab your needles and some yarn, then stick with me as I talk you through the basic techniques.

Holding the needles

If you are a beginner, the first question you are probably wondering is, 'How do I hold my knitting needles?' There is no right or wrong answer, but I would always advise trying some different techniques and seeing what feels most natural to you. Don't be afraid to hold them in your own way! The most common ways to hold the needles are:

Like a knife

Pick up the needles with your hands resting lightly on top of the needles and tips pointing towards each other. Your hands should be near the tips of the needles, but not right at the ends. This is the way I hold my needles. The downside of this holding style is that you have to lift your right hand off the needle to wrap the yarn around the tip of the needle, so it can be a bit slower and harder to maintain an even tension.

Like a pencil

Hold the working needle as if you are holding a pencil, with your thumb and forefinger lightly gripping the needle close to the pointed tip and the shaft resting at the base of your thumb, with the tips pointing towards each other. Hold the needle that contains the stitches about to be worked with the 'knife' grip. With this technique, you do not need to let go of the needles when working a stitch but simply slide your right hand forward to manipulate the yarn. With this holding style, it can be easier to maintain an even tension and constant flow of yarn.

Holding the yarn

Just as there is no single right way to hold the needles, there are different ways of holding the yarn around your fingers to control the tension, so you can produce even stitches. The aim is to achieve a constant flow of yarn that is neither too tight or too loose. You can hold the yarn in either your left or right hand.

Holding the yarn in your right hand

Holding the yarn in your right hand (or RH) is called the English style or 'throwing' and most beginners find this way the easiest to learn. Hold the needle that is carrying the stitches in your left hand (or LH) and the wrap the yarn around your fingers in one of the following three ways.

Method one: With your palm upwards, wind the yarn over the little finger of your RH, under your third finger, then over your centre finger and under your index finger. When knitting, use your RH index finger to wrap the yarn around the point of the needle to work a stitch and control the tension of the yarn.

Method two: With your palm upwards, wind the yarn around the little finger of your RH, under your third finger, then over your centre finger and under your index finger. When knitting, use your RH index finger to wrap the yarn around the point of the needle to work a stitch and control the tension of the yarn.

Method three: With your palm upwards, wind the yarn around the little finger of your RH, over your third and centre fingers, then around your index finger. When knitting, use your RH index finger to wrap the yarn around the point of the needle to work a stitch and control the tension of the yarn.

Holding the yarn in your left hand

Holding the yarn in your left hand (LH) is called the Continental style or 'picking'. Hold the needle that is carrying the stitches in your RH, then wind the yarn around your fingers in one of the following ways.

Method one: With your palm upwards, wind the yarn around the little finger of your LH, over the third and centre fingers, then under your index finger. When knitting, use your LH index finger to wrap the yarn around the point of the needle to work a stitch and control the tension of the yarn.

Method two: With your palm upwards, wind the yarn around the little finger of your LH, under the third finger, over the centre finger, then under your index finger. When knitting, use your LH index finger to wrap the yarn around the point of the needle to work a stitch and control the tension of the yarn.

(TOM'S TIP:)

```
The way you knit is exactly the same
whatever yarn holding technique you
choose to use. Always use the way
that feels most comfortable to you.
I have the yarn running between my
index and third fingers to control
the tension and let the yarn run
through my hand. I just find this
the most natural way for me.
```

Making a slip knot

Almost every knitting project starts with a slip knot, which is counted as the first cast-on stitch. The slip knot acts as an anchor for the rest of your knitting.

One: With the yarn end on your right, unwind about 15cm (6 inches) from the ball. Make a loop by forming an upside-down U-shape and folding the right side goes over the left side. Place the yarn at the back of your loop.

Two: Put your fingers through the loop making it larger and pull through the yarn to form another U. Slip the loop onto your needle and pull the tail of the yarn so the knot lies at the base of the loop – this is your slipknot.

Three: Pull the yarn that is attached to the ball to tighten the slipknot, and you're ready to start knitting.

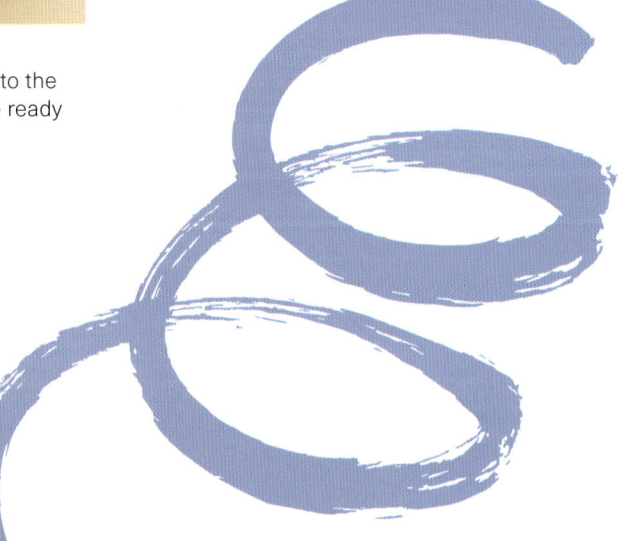

Casting on

Casting on is the term used to describe putting the first row of stitches onto your needles, so you can start creating your masterpiece. There are many ways to cast on, so ask a few different knitters and they will give you different ways to cast on. Some are worked with one needle and others are worked with two. Whatever method you use, do not cast on too tightly; your stitches should be able to move freely up and down your needle.

Thumb cast-on method

This is one of the easiest ways to cast on. It is done with just one needle and produces a cast-on edge that has good elasticity.

One: Start with a slipknot and place it on the RH needle leaving a yarn end with enough length to make all the stitches (around 2.5cm or 1 inch) per stitch. With the needle in your RH grab the yarn tail (not attached to the ball) with your LH, making a thumbs-up sign. Wind your thumb behind the yarn.

Two: Touch the needle to the front of your thumb and slide the tip into the loop from the bottom. Wrap the working end of the yarn (attached to the ball) around the needle in an anti-clockwise direction (from the back to the front).

Three: Slide the loop on your thumb up and over the tip of the needle, then slip your thumb out of the loop.

Four: Pull the yarn tail to tighten up the new stitch. Repeat until you have the required number of stitches on your needle.

Knitting Essentials

Cable cast-on method

This cast-on method is a specific way of casting on stitches when you are going on to work in stocking stitch. It makes a neat, firm and decorative edge, which makes it ideal for projects like cosy blankets.

One: Make a slipknot and place it on your LH needle. With the working end of the yarn in your RH, put the tip of the RH needle into the stitch on the LH needle. Wrap the yarn around the RH needle anti-clockwise and draw it through to the front as if to knit, but do not slip the stitch off the end of the needle.

Two: Bring the RH needle towards you and pull on the stitch to make it a little larger. Transfer the new stitch to the LH needle – you now have two stitches.

Three: To make the next stitch, put the tip of the RH needle between the two stitches on the LH needle. Wrap the yarn anti-clockwise round the RH needle again, then draw it through to the front.

Four: Pull the needle towards you as before and transfer this stitch onto the LH needle – you now have three stitches. Repeat the last two steps until you have the right number of stitches on your needle.

Long-tail cast-on method

This is my favourite way of casting on because I think it is the quickest and most secure. It provides a firm and elastic edge and is also a good way for beginners to learn. I also think it looks really neat.

One: Make a slipknot and place it on your RH needle, leaving a long tail of yarn. Ensure the tail is facing towards you and insert your LH thumb and index finger between the two strands of yarn.

Two: Close your fingers around the yarn and insert the RH needle under the loop of the strand that is wrapped around your thumb.

Three: Then scoop up the loop that has been formed around your index finger and bring it down.

Four: Bring your yarn out through the thumb loop and tighten the loop on the needle to form the new stitch.

Knitting Essentials

Basic stitches →

Once you have cast on some stitches, you can now start to knit. There are two main stitches within knitting – the knit stitch and the purl stitch. These two stitches can be worked in different combinations to create various textures or knitted fabrics, or stitch patterns.

Knit stitch   The knit stitch is the basis of most other stitch patterns – a bit like a front dive, I guess! Learn this one and you will be a pro-knitter in no time. In any pattern, knit is abbreviated to k, so k1 means knit one stitch, while k1 row translates to knit one row.

One: Hold the needle with the cast-on stitches in your left hand (LH) with the working yarn (attached to the ball) at the back of the needle. This should be approx. 2.5cm (1 inch) from the tip of the needle. Insert the point of the right hand (RH) needle into the first stitch on the LH needle, from front to back and under the LH needle.

Two: Wrap the yarn around the point of the RH needle, in an anti-clockwise direction (from the back to the front), so the yarn slides between the two needles.

Three: Pull the RH needle towards you and slip the tip under the LH needle to form a loop – you now have one loop on the RH needle. Slide the stitch just worked off the LH needle by gently pulling the RH needle to your right.

Four: Gently tighten the yarn as necessary. Repeat until you have a full row of knit stitches on the RH needle. Start a new row by transferring the needle holding the stitches back into your LH and creating a new row of stitches on the RH needle.

TOM'S TIP:

```
For left-handers, you need to reverse the right-handed knit stitch, so
move the yarn from the right to the left by wrapping the yarn clockwise –
instead of anti-clockwise. The yarn should be at the back and you should
end the stitch from front to back.
```

Knitting Essentials

Purl stitch The purl stitch is an equally important stitch. Purl is abbreviated to p, so p1 means purl one stitch. If you purl every row, the finished fabric will look the same as knitting every row, except the process is much slower.

One: Hold the needle with the cast-on stitches in your LH, with the working yarn (attached to the ball) at the front of the needle. Insert the tip of the RH needle into the first stitch on the LH needle, from back to front (rather than front to back as with the knit stitch).

Two: Wrap the yarn around the RH needle in an anti-clockwise direction, finishing with the yarn in front of your needles again.

Three: Slide the RH needle down and behind the tip of the LH. Slide the stitch just worked off the LH needle by gently pulling the RH needle to your right.

Four: Gently tighten the yarn as necessary. Repeat until you have a full row of purl stitches on the RH needle. Start a new row by transferring the needle holding the stitches back into your LH and creating a new row of stitches on the RH needle.

Joining in a new ball of yarn

When you have finished one ball of yarn, you will need to add a new ball to carry on knitting. It is the same technique used as when you are re-joining yarn to stitches held on a stitch holder or starting a different colour and it is always best to make the change at the end of a row, leaving a tail of about 10cm (4 inches).

One: Place your work down and make a cross shape with the new yarn under the old working yarn. Loosely tie the new yarn in a knot around the old yarn. Slide the knot up until it is next to the knitting needle. Tighten the knot by pulling both ends of the yarn.

Two: Start knitting with your new yarn – easy! Where you have added in a new yarn or changed colour, you will be left with loose yarn ends that will need to be sewn into your knitting to secure them, so they don't unravel (see page 78).

TOM'S TIP:

When you're first learning to knit, count your stitches after each row to ensure that your knitting is correct and you haven't dropped any stitches. Always complete an entire row of stitches before putting your needles down. So, if someone calls or WhatsApps you, don't be tempted to answer as it's quite likely that you'll forget where you were.

Increasing and decreasing →

Increasing and decreasing stitches means adding or reducing the number of stitches to increase or decrease the width of your knitting, which can give it an angled shape or turn a flat fabric into something more three-dimensional. So, if you are making a sweater or cardigan, for example, this will help to shape it. Increasing and decreasing can also add an attractive detail to your design.

Increasing

Some methods of increasing stitches make more of a visual impact than others. The most popular ways are knit front and back (kfb) and make one (m1). The main difference is that with kfb two stitches are made from one existing stitch and m1 makes the increase from the horizontal strand between two existing stitches. The results look quite different, so it is important to use whatever increase has been specified in the pattern to ensure that the finished item looks like the designer intended. I know increasing might sound terrifying, but once you have done it a few times, you will soon get the hang of it!

Knit front and back (kfb or inc)

This increase turns one stitch into two by knitting into both the front and back of the loop. However, it does leave a visible bar of yarn across the base of the increased stitch, which is why it is also known as a bar increase. This method of increasing is commonly used in sweater patterns, but it creates a slight hole where the increase is worked and so is best worked on the edge where the knitting will be incorporated into a seam.

One: Make a knit stitch in the front of the next stitch on the LH needle in the usual way, but do not slide off the original stitch.

Two: Then insert the RH needle through the back loop of the same stitch on the LH needle.

Three: Bring the yarn from behind and wrap it around the point of the RH needle in an anti-clockwise direction. Draw the yarn through the loop by going into and out of the stitch (in the same way you would make a knit stitch).

Four: Slide the original stitch off the LH needle – you now have two stitches.

Purl front and back (pfb or inc)

As with the equivalent technique on a knit row, this increasing method on a purl row leaves a visible bar at the base of the stitch and a slight hole, so again, it is best worked on the edges of a garment where it will disappear into a side seam.

One: Make a purl stitch in the front of the next stitch on the LH needle in the usual way, but do not slide the original stitch off the LH needle.

Two: Angle the RH needle backwards, then insert it through the back loop of the same stitch on the LH needle.

Three: Wrap the yarn around the point of the RH needle in an anti-clockwise direction. Draw the yarn through the loop by going into and out of the stitch (in the same way you would make a purl stitch), then slide the original stitch off the LH needle. You have now increased by one stitch.

Make one (m1)

This increase is made by making use of the bar in between two stitches. A make-one-left (m1l) picks up the loop front to back and knits through the back loop. A make-one right (m1r) picks up the loop from back to front and knits through the front loop. Some patterns do not state which method to use, so check to ensure you are using the best increase method.

Make one left (m1l) on knit row

One: Insert the LH needle under the horizontal strand running between two stitches from front to back. Lift it onto the LH needle.

Two: Insert the RH needle knitwise into the back of the loop formed by the lifted strand. Knit that loop as you would through the back loop. You have now increased by one stitch.

Make one right (m1r) on knit row

One: Insert the LH needle under the horizontal strand running between two stitches from back to front. Lift it onto the LH needle.

Two: Insert the RH needle knitwise into the front of the loop formed by the lifted strand. Knit that loop as you would knit a regular stitch. You have now increased by one stitch.

Knitting Essentials

Decreasing

In the same way you shape garments by increasing stitches, there will be times you need to decrease to shape your project. As a general rule, decreases are made so that they slope in the same direction as the edge of the knitted fabric for a neat look.

Knit two together (k2tog)

The most common way of decreasing is to knit together two adjacent stitches at the same time to leave one stitch. This is called knit two together (k2tog) and creates a decrease that slopes to the right. You can also purl two together (p2tog). This can be done at the start, end, or middle of a row.

One: Instead of inserting the tip of the RH needle into one stitch, insert it into two stitches at the same time, from left to right.

Two: Wrap the yarn around the RH needle just as you would when knitting a single stitch. Draw the loop of working yarn through both stitches.

Three: Complete the stitch as normal by dropping both stitches off the LH needle. You have now decreased by one stitch.

Knit two together through back loops (k2togtbl)

This way to decrease is similar to k2tog, except you knit into the back of the stitches. It creates a decrease that slopes to the left. You can also purl two together through the back loop (p2togtbl), which is the corresponding right-leaning version of p2tog.

One: Instead of inserting the tip of the RH needle into one stitch, insert it into two stitches at the same time at the back of the work, from right to left.

Two: Wrap the yarn around the RH needle just as you would when knitting a single stitch. Complete the stitch as normal, leaving just one stitch on the RH needle.

Purl two together through back loops (p2tog tbl)

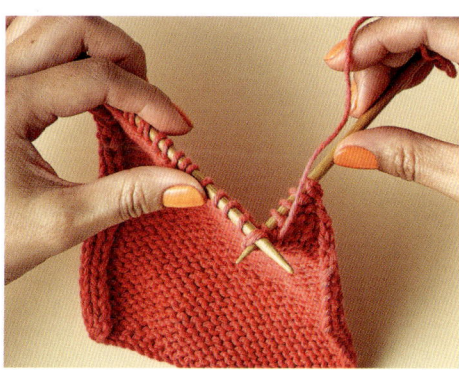

One: Insert the tip of the RH needle through two stitches at the same time at the back of the work, from left to right.

Two: Wrap the yarn around the RH needle just as you would when knitting a single stitch. Complete the stitch as normal, leaving just one stitch on the RH needle.

Knitting Essentials

Slip one, knit one, pass slipped stitch over (s1 k1 psso)

Whereas k2tog creates a decrease that slopes to the right, this method of decreasing slants to the left and so k2tog and k2tog tbl are often used in tandem on opposite sides of a garment to create symmetrical shaping.

One: Insert the RH needle knitwise into the next stitch on the LH needle and slip it onto the RH needle.

Two: Knit the next stitch on the LH needle in the usual way.

Three: Using the LH needle, lift the slipped stitch on the RH needle over the stitch just knitted, then slide it off both needles. You have now decreased by one stitch.

Slip slip knit (ssk) This is another left-sloping decrease and the mirror image of k2tog. You can also slip slip purl (ssp), which is the mirror image of a p2tog. This can be done at the start, end, or middle of a row.

One: Slip two stitches knitwise from the LH needle onto the RH needle without knitting them.

Two: Insert the LH needle in the front loops of these stitches. Wrap the yarn the normal way around the RH needle and knit the two stitches together to form one stitch.

Slip slip purl (ssp)

One: Slip two stitches purlwise from the LH needle onto the RH needle without purling them.

Two: Insert the LH needle in the front loops of these stitches. Wrap the yarn the normal way around the RH needle and purl the two stitches together to form one stitch.

Casting off →

You've made it to the end and finished a piece of knitting? Well done! Casting off, as it is known in the UK, or binding off if you are in the U.S., is the term used for creating an end to your knitting so the stitches can be secured and will not unravel. Over the next few pages are the most common ways to cast off, which I use all the time.

(KNITTING)

Casting-off (binding off) knitwise

One: To cast off (bind off), start a new row and knit two stitches. Remember that it has to be two stitches!

Two: Slide the LH needle into the first stitch that has just been knitted. Lift it over the second stitch and off the needle. There is now one stitch on your RH needle – the other one has been cast off (bound off).

Three: Knit one more stitch so you have two stitches on your RH needle and repeat the process. When you only have one stitch left, cut off the yarn giving it at least a 15-cm (6-inch) tail.

Four: Pull the stitch over the yarn tail and pull the tail all the way through. Tighten it all up to secure. Depending on what the piece is for, the long yarn end can be used to sew together the project.

Casting off (binding off) purlwise

Depending on the pattern you are working from, you may be instructed to cast off (bind off) on a purl row, in which case you will need to work purl stitches that are then lifted over each other in the same way as casting off knitwise.

One: Start by purling two stitches in the usual way. Slide the LH needle into the first purled stitch from left to right, at the back of the work. Bring it over the top of the second stitch and off the needle.

Two: There is now one stitch on your RH needle – the other one has been cast off (bound off). Purl one more stitch so you have two stitches on your RH needle and repeat this process until you have one stitch left. Fasten off as for a knitwise cast off (bind off).

When casting off (binding off) try to not do it too tightly, so keep your tension on your right needle looser than you would when knitting normally. Alternatively, go up a needle size to give the edge a bit more elasticity.

Casting off (binding off) on three needles

This is a useful technique when you need to cast off (bind off) two pieces of knitting together, for example to create a neat shoulder seam.

One: Hold the two pieces of knitting together in your left hand with their right sides touching. The points of the needles should be parallel and facing in the same direction. Using a third needle, slide the point of this needle into the first stitch of the knitting on the front needle and then into the first stitch of the knitting on the back needle.

Two: Wrap the working yarn from the front piece anti-clockwise around the tip of the third needle, then draw the loop through both stitches at the same time. Drop the stitches just knitted off their respective needles, leaving the new stitch on the third needle. Knit the next two stitches in the same way, so you now have two stitches on the third needle.

Three: Using the tip of one of the needles in your left hand, pass the first stitch on the third needle over the second stitch and drop that stitch off the third needle just as if you were casting off (binding off) knitwise.

Four: Knit the next two stitches from the front and back pieces together as before and repeat all the steps until you have one stitch left. Fasten off in the same way as for a knitwise cast off (bind off).

Stitch patterns every knitter should know →

The knit stitch and the purl stitch form the basis of all the other patterns and textures within knitting — you just need to know how to combine them to achieve the effect you want.

Go-to easy stitch patterns

Having the knit stitch and purl stitch in your locker opens up a whole range of stitch patterns, especially when they are used in conjunction with increases, decreases and yarn overs. Here are some of the most common ones to kickstart your repertoire.

Garter stitch

This stitch is created by knitting every row. It forms a ridged pattern that is the same on both sides, other than at the cast-on edge. This is the perfect stitch for your first attempt at knitting and can be used in many different ways to create beautiful knitting. It creates a series of wave-like ridges, created with interlocking stitch loops. If your pattern does not tell you, you can choose your RS and for me, this is normally the side that has the first row of knitted stitches.

Stocking (stockinette) stitch

This is my favourite stitch pattern. It reminds me of my Christmas stocking when I was a kid. Stocking stitch, or stockinette stitch, is created by alternately knitting and purling rows. It creates different textures on each side of the work. The knit side is flat with small 'V's – this is the front or the right side (RS). The purl side is ridged and is the back or the wrong side (WS). Stocking stitch shows off the quality of the yarn, so it is often used for colourwork. With stocking stitch, the fabric naturally curls in at the edges, so it is often deliberately used to create rolled cuffs or hems, instead of rib.

Reverse stocking (stockinette) stitch

This is worked in the same way as stocking (stockinette) stitch except that you purl the first row and knit the second, so the front of the fabric is the ridged purl side and the back is the smooth knit side.

Moss (seed) stitch

Moss (seed) stitch is made up of single knit and purl stitches alternating both horizontally and vertically. This creates a versatile textured fabric that lies flat and is fully reversible, so it is popular for all sorts of items.

(TOM'S TIP:)

What is known as moss stitch in the UK is called seed stitch in the U.S. If an American pattern calls for seed stitch or a British pattern tells you to work moss stitch, it is exactly the same thing. I know - can feel a bit confusing!

Rib stitches

Rib stitch is a textured vertical stripe pattern that is used for flexible, elastic necklines, hems and cuffs on garments, as well as scarves and hats. It is made by knitting and purling stitches in one row, then purling and knitting the same stitches in the next row to create alternate columns of knit and purl stitches. The different types of rib stitches are worked using varying combinations – any pattern will tell you what combination of stitches to work and in what order. Rib stitches create a lovely stretchy fabric. The stretchiness will depend on the column width – the narrower the column the stretchier the fabric.

Single rib stitch (1x1 rib)

Single rib stitch, which is often abbreviated to 1x1 rib, alternates single knit stitches with single purl stitches, creating thin columns. The main thing to remember as you alternate stitches is to move the yarn after each stitch: it needs to be at the back of your knitting for each knit stitch and at the front for every purl stitch worked.

Double rib stitch (2x2 rib)

Double rib stitch, or 2x2 rib, alternates two knit stitches with two purl stitches. This creates a fabric that is slightly less stretchy than single rib stitch. This stitch pattern is best worked over a multiple of four stitches.

TOM'S TIP:

If you don't take the yarn forwards and backwards between the rib stitches, you will be left with extra loops lying across the needle. Count your stitches carefully at the end of each row and if there are too many, this might have happened!

Reading a knitting pattern →

Once you have tackled the basics – casting on, knit, purl, and casting off (binding off) – you'll be ready to start your first project. The first time I tried to follow a knitting pattern, it looked completely incomprehensible. However, over time I got the hang of deciphering the instructions. There are loads of abbreviations and terms used In knitting patterns, but once you have used them a few times, they are super-easy to understand.

KNITTING

Understanding knitting abbreviations

Knitting patterns commonly use abbreviations, which makes them quicker to read. So, k is knit, p is purl, co is cast on, and so on. Any abbreviation outside of the norm used within a specific pattern are usually included at the start of the instructions.

General

Instructions are written using UK terminology with the U.S. terminology given in round brackets ( ) afterwards

[ ] instructions are given for the smallest size first, with changes for the larger sizes given in order within square brackets afterwards

( ) work any instructions within round brackets as many times as directed afterwards

* repeat instructions following the single asterisk as many times as directed afterwards

* * repeat instructions between asterisks as many times as directed or from a given set of instructions

alt alternate
approx. approximately
beg begin or beginning
bet between
cc contrast colour
circ circular
cm centimetre(s)
cn cable needle
CO cast on
cont continue
dec decrease or decreasing
dpns double-pointed needles
foll follow or following
g gram(s)
gt st garter stitch
in inch(es)
inc increase or increasing
k knit

k1b knit stitch in row below
kfb knit into front and back of a stitch – single knit increase
k2tog knit two stitches together
k2tog tbl knit two stitches together through back loops
kwise knitwise
LH lefthand
m marker
m1 or m1k make one stitch or make one stitch knitwise by picking up and knitting into back of loop between stitch just worked and next stitch – single knit increase
m1r make one right – right-leaning knit increase
m1l make one left – left-leaning knit increase
m1p make one purlwise
m1rp make one right – right-leaning purl increase
m1lp make one left – left-leaning purl increase
mb make bobble
mc main colour
meas measure(s)
oz ounce(s)
p purl
p2tog purl two stitches together
p2tog tbl purl two stitches together through back loops
patt pattern
pfb purl into front and back of a stitch – single purl increase
pm place marker
prev previous
psso pass slipped stitch over

p2sso pass two slipped stitches over
pwise purlwise
rem remain or remaining
rep repeat
Rev St st reverse stocking (stockinette) stitch
RH righthand
rnd round
RS right side
skp slip next stitch, knit next stitch, pass slipped stitch over the knit stitch
sl1k slip one stitch knitwise
sl2k slip two stitches knitwise
sl1p slip one stitch purlwise
sl2p slip two stitches purlwise
sl st slip stitch
sm slip marker
ssk slip next two stitches separately knitwise then insert lefthand needle through front of these two stitches and knit together
ssp slip slip purl
st(s) stitch(es)
St st Stocking (stockinette) stitch
tbl through back loop
tfl through front loop
tog together
WS wrong side
wyab with yarn at back
wyif with yarn in front
yb yarn to back of work between needles
yds yards
yfwd yarn to front of work between needles
yo yarn over
yon yarn over needle

Knitting Essentials

Reading a knitting pattern

Think of it like following a recipe – it makes sense to have everything you need to hand before you cast on and get started. Some patterns use slightly different writing styles and I have tried to keep mine as straightforward as possible.

Most commercial knitting patterns follow this format:

1. Skill level: Some patterns advise the skill level. As a beginner, I recommend starting with scarves and blankets that are relatively easy to build confidence. The first item I completed was my simple red and white striped sweater. The first few patterns in this book are designed to get you started from scratch.

2. Measurements: If the pattern is for a garment, there is usually a range of sizes given in a chart from which to choose based on the measurements given. If a project is one-size then the finished dimensions are shown.

3. What you will need: This tells you the type of yarn, standard yarn weight, meterage (yardage) and number of balls needed to complete the project, plus any other equipment, like stitch markers, a cable needle and a yarn needle.

4. Tension (gauge): This is the recommended number of stitches and rows in a certain area, usually 10cm (4 inch) square. Achieving the recommended tension given in the instructions is especially important when making garments.

5. Abbreviations: This gives you the key to unlock all the abbreviations used in the pattern.

6. Special techniques: This highlights any particular techniques used within the design, and refers you to the pages where they are explained in detail.

7. Pattern instructions: This is either written out line-by-line or presented in chart form with a key alongside to decode the chart. Designers will aim to give you the right information and tips in order to make your work a success

8. Finishing instructions: This tells you how to complete your project, including sewing up seams and adding any other decorative touches.

Balloon Sleeve Cardigan

1 EASY

A simple edge-to-edge cardigan with dramatic balloon-shaped cuffs, this easy to knit project creates a big impact. Designed to be cropped to sit at the waist, for a flattering fit. I love the back neck detail where the two fronts meet at the centre of the back neck for a neat and comfortable finish when worn.

2 **Measurements**
See chart below

3 **What you will need**
- Debbie Bliss Nell
  78% mohair, 13% merino wool, 9% polyamide
  100m (109 yards) per 50g (1¾ oz)

Quantity:
- 7[7:8:9:9] x 50g (1¾ oz) balls in Lilac
- 1 pair 6mm (US 10) knitting needles
- Stitch markers
- Stitch holders
- Yarn needle

4 **Tension (gauge)**
13 sts and 17 rows to 10cm (4 in) over St st stitch using 6mm (US 10) needles. Change needle size as necessary to achieve correct tension (gauge).

5 **Abbreviations**
See page 69.

6 **Special technique**
Short-row shaping (see pages 102–103).

Adult size	XS	S/M	L/XL	XXL	XXXL	
To fit chest	71–86	91.5–106.5	111.5–117	122–137	142–156	cm
	28–34	36–42	44–46	48–54	56–61	in
Actual chest	117	126	138.5	147.5	157	cm
	46	49½	54½	58	61¾	in
Length	50	52	54	56	58	cm
	19¾	20½	21¼	22	22¾	in
Sleeve length	45	45	45	43	43	cm
	17¾	17¾	17¾	17	17	in

Working from a chart

Charts are visual representations of knitting instructions. They condense more complex stitch and colourwork patterns, so they take up less space than if the instructions were written out row-by-row. They are particularly useful for designs like colour motifs, intarsia (a colourwork technique that involves knitting in blocks of colour, see page 149) and Fair Isle (a traditional knitting technique used to create patterns in multiple colours, see page 131). Some designers will provide both written instructions and a chart. Charts also help you to envisage how the finished piece should look so you can identify where you are as you knit – and spot any mistake sooner.

Charts can be really helpful as you learn to knit. The chart will be laid out as a grid, with little cells like graph paper. These cells are not square but wider than they are tall to reflect the proportions of the knit stitch.

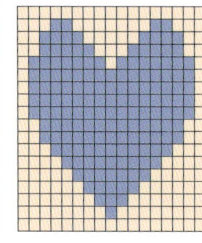

The two charts above show how different a simple heart motif looks when knitted versus when drawn out on square graph paper. This is important if you decide to create your own motif. You can buy special knitter's chart paper or create your own.

Each cell in a chart represents one knitted stitch and will either be filled with colour or have a symbol inside it to denote a colour or texture stitch. Each horizontal line of cells represents one knitted row. Every chart is accompanied by a key that tells you what each colour or symbol denotes.

So, the question is: How do you read a knitting chart? The first clue: Not like a book! A chart shows how your work will look on the right side. The pattern instructions will clearly state when you need to start working from any chart, how to place it within your knitting, how much of the chart to work and whether it needs to be repeated. The very first stitch of the motif or pattern is usually worked on a right side row, so it is represented by the cell at the bottom righthand corner of the chart, but it can be the bottom lefthand corner if you begin working from the chart on a wrong side row.

It is always a good idea to take the time to read any pattern and chart instructions before you start knitting, so you know what to expect, but at the same time don't overthink it. Take it row by row and it will all start to make sense and fall into place.

- Pay attention to any key provided – different patterns may use varying symbols.

- Start reading from the bottom of the chart and work your way up.

- Right side rows are always read from right to left.

- Wrong side rows are always read from left to right.

- When working in the round, every row is a right side row read from right to left.

- Mark off each row as you complete it. Some knitters use removable highlighter tape or sticky notes to show their place. I just tick them off in pencil as I go.

Patterns may use a repeat section, so if your chart has only 16 cells in a single row and yet you need to work 64 stitches in a row, do not panic! When a colour motif or stitch pattern is repeated several times across a knitted row, often it is only the repeated section that is charted, plus any extra stitches at the start and end of the rows. The pattern repeat is clearly indicated, usually by lines or arrows pointing to the repeated stitches. These stitches are worked across the row as many times as needed, while those stitches outside the repeat are worked just once either at the start or end of the row. The instructions will tell you where to place the pattern within your work and how many times to work the repeat across a row and for how many rows. If the repeat extends across the width of the chart, simply work from edge to edge.

Colour motif chart and key

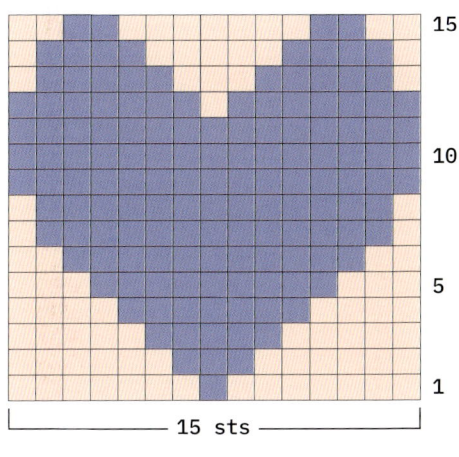

Key:
A k on RS, p on WS
B k on RS, p on WS

Stitch pattern chart and key

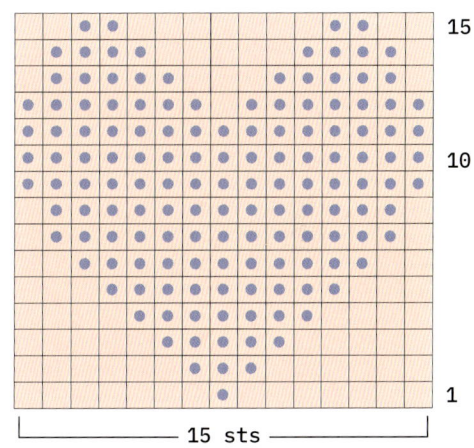

Key:
A k on RS, p on WS
B p on RS, k on WS

Repeat pattern chart and key

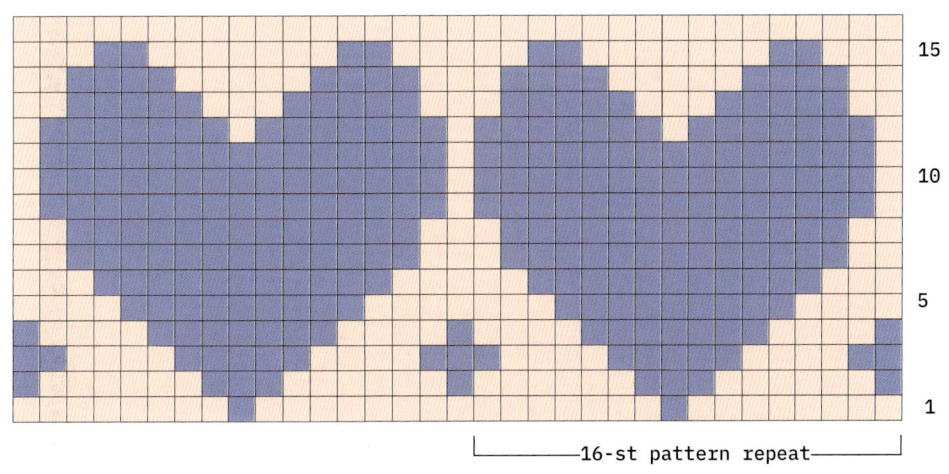

Knitting Essentials

Working a tension or gauge swatch

I know it's tempting to dive straight into creating something new, but before you start you will need to knit a tension or gauge swatch. This will tell you how many stitches and rows you need to work to produce a 10-cm or 4-inch square to achieve the same dimensions in your work as the pattern designer intended. Before you start any project, this is a way to determine whether you need to work more tightly or loosely if the item you're making requires an exact fit.

For complete beginners, you could skip this bit for any patterns that do not need precise dimensions. However, it is good practice to get into the habit of completing a tension (gauge) swatch as it is an essential part of the making process. It is useful to learn to how to adjust your tension (gauge) even though it can feel a bit tedious at times.

If the pattern states the number of stitches and rows measured over 10cm (4 inches), always work a tension swatch at least a few centimetres (an inch) larger as often side stitches can be tighter than the main fabric. For this reason, take the measurement from the centre of the swatch.

Lay your swatch flat or block it without stretching it. Measure a 10-cm (4-inch) section, both horizontally and vertically, marking the edges of the area with pins. Now count the number of stitches and rows inside the two pins. If it meets the number given in the pattern instructions, then great! If not, you may need to go up a needle size if you are a tight knitter, or down a size, if you are a loose knitter.

The general rule is that one difference in needle size will create a difference of one stitch in the tension (gauge). Knit the swatch again to check you are on track. Every knitter's work is different, so every garment will end up looking and fitting slightly differently, but to me this is one of the best things about knitting. Practice really does make perfect!

(TOM'S TIP:)

Once you have made a tension or gauge swatch with a certain type of yarn and size of needles, create a label for it, with this information. Often patterns will call for the same yarn and needles, so you won't always have to knit a new tension or gauge swatch for every project. Once you have finished with the swatches, you could patchwork them together to make something new, like a scarf or a blanket.

Troubleshooting tips →

We all have moments when our knitting goes wrong, but don't worry – fixing mistakes can be easier than you may fear! I've made loads of mistakes in my work and each time every one was different. I think that embracing your mistakes and learning from them is all part of the making process.

KNITTING

Picking up a dropped stitch

We've all been there. You're happily knitting when you notice a dreaded 'ladder' where a stitch has slipped off the needle. My first tip is don't panic! As soon as you notice it, lay your piece flat, so you can see exactly what is going on. If you have dropped a stitch while doing stocking (stockinette) stitch, it is easier to correct with the knit side facing.

Picking up one stitch over one row on knit side

One: If you have noticed one dropped stitch on stocking (stockinette) stitch, it will look something like this.

Two: Insert the RH needle into the loop of the dropped stitch and under the strand of the yarn below, so both the strand and stitch are on the needle.

Three: Insert LH needle from front to back and pull the stitch over the strand.

Four: You have corrected your dropped stitch! Put the stitch on your LH needle, so you can continue.

Picking up edge stitches

Because the first stitch on the needle is usually the loosest and the one nearest the point of the needle, it is often the stitch that gets dropped most frequently. When an edge stitch has been dropped, it will have been dropped by two rows rather than one and so a large loop of yarn will be visible. The simplest way to pick up and re-make these loops into stitches is to use a crochet hook and work from the right side of the fabric.

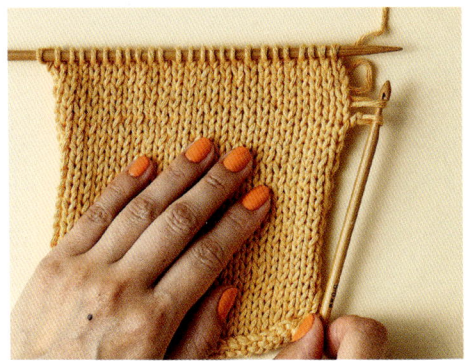

One: Insert a crochet hook into the dropped stitch and catch the large loop of yarn.

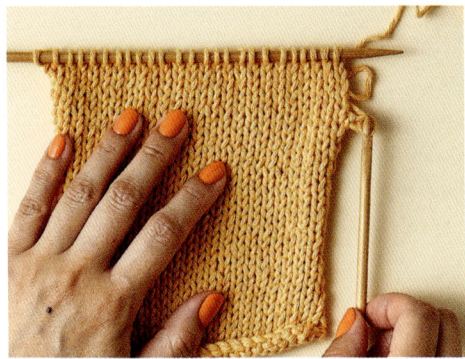

Two: Draw the yarn through the dropped stitch, but only a loop that is the size of a single stitch; don't pull the whole of the large loop through. You have re-made one stitch.

Three: Catch the large loop again and draw a second loop through the stitch on the hook; this is the second re-made stitch and the last one to be made from the large loop. If there is more than one large loop, re-make them all into stitches in this way, making two stitches from each large loop.

Four: At the top, the final re-made stitch is made from the working yarn. Pull a loop of the yarn through the stitch on the crochet hook, then place this last stitch back onto the knitting needle, making sure it is facing the right way.

Extra stitches

From time to time, you may find yourself looking at your knitting thinking, 'Hmmm, that looks like too many stitches'. You might notice holes or the sides of your fabric slanting upwards. It's a common beginner mistake and might happen from accidental yarn overs or knitting between stitches. The best way to stop this from happening is to look at your knitting carefully from time to time and also to count your stitches repeatedly. Just admire your work regularly!

One: If the extra stitch was a yarn over within the last two rows or you notice that there are too many stitches in the middle of the row no more than few rows back, the best idea is to simply unravel and reknit.

Two: Always check the first stitch of a row before you start knitting. If it has swivelled upwards on the needle it may look like it is two stitches, so be sure to knit the stitch on the needle, not the two strands below.

Incomplete stitch on knit row

One: You may spot an incomplete stitch. The right part of the stitch will look baggy and there will be a hole. Pick up your knitting normally and knit up to the incomplete stitch.

Two: To fix it take your RH needle and insert it through the front of the left part of the incomplete stitch – this can be a bit fiddly, so persevere. Transfer the yarn up and over the right part of the incomplete stitch and slide the RH needle out so the stitch sits on the LH needle. This fixes the stitch and you can continue knitting.

Knitting Essentials

Twisted stitches

If you think of a stitch as having two legs – the right leg should be at the front, with the left leg behind. This should be the same regardless of whether you are working in knit stitch or purl stitch. If you notice a twisted stitch, the chances are that you wrapped the yarn the wrong way around your needle or you put your stitch back on your needle the wrong way round. So, what can you do about it?

Twisted stitch on knit row

One: Look at your row of knit stitches. If the right leg of any stitch is sitting behind the left leg, then the stitch is twisted.

Two: Work up to your twisted stitch and take the stitch off the LH needle and correct its position, then transfer it back onto the LH needle.

Unpicking stitches one by one

Wrong stitch or in the wrong place? Don't stress! All sorts of mistakes mean you may have to unpick your knitting. Unpicking one stitch at a time is called 'tinking', which means 'backwards knitting'. Cute name!

One: Before starting a new row, check over the row just worked for any errors – here one stitch has become twisted on the needle, meaning that right leg of the stitch is sitting to the back of the needle rather than the front. The easiest thing to do it to unpick the stitches one by one up to the error in order to re-knit it.

Two: Holding the needle carrying the stitches in your LH, insert the tip of the RH needle into the row directly below the one on the LH needle that you want to unravel. Carefully drop the stitch off the LH needle and pull the yarn towards you so that the stitch of the row below transfers to the RH needle. Repeat this until you reach the error that you have identified.

Unravelling rows

If all else fails, you may need to unravel your knitting for a few rows. You can either freestyle and unravel your yarn and knitting to the point beyond the mistake and pick up the loose stitches with your needles, or you can do it in a more controlled way, using a 'lifeline' – a length of yarn that you thread through a lower row or round. This means you do not need to worry about unravelling too far, dropping stitches, or getting them twisted. It is an excellent way to rescue your knitting if you have made a mistake. Unravelling your work is called ripping out or frogging. It's a bit nerve-racking at first but gets easier after you have done it a few times.

One: Thread a yarn needle with a length of waste yarn in a contrast colour to the work. Pass the needle through the front of each stitch in the row to which you want to unravel.

Two: Slide the knitting off the knitting needle. Now pull out the yarn to unravel the knitting row by row until you reach the lifeline. The lifeline will stop the work from unravelling further and hold the stitches in a row facing the right direction to be picked up.

Three: Following the lifeline, slip each stitch back onto the knitting needle, pulling out the yarn as you go. Check that the working yarn is at the tip of the knitting needle, then you can start knitting again.

(TOM'S TIP:)

```
It can be great practice to put
regular lifelines into your work
as a preventative measure. If you
make a mistake, simply unravel
your knitting to the lifeline and
continue. Lifelines can be anything
- a contrasting colour yarn, string,
or ribbon! It is better if the
lifeline is thinner than the yarn
you are working with though, so it
does not stretch out the stitches
that it is threaded through.
```

Knitting Essentials

Finishing your makes →

Now it's time to work some magic and turn your knitted fabric into something special. After investing a lot of your time in knitting the pieces, how you apply the final touches to a project makes a huge difference. A whole book could be written about how to sew up and finish items, but here I cover the most useful basic techniques to learn, so you can make your items look gorgeous. As with anything knitting-related, the more you practise, the easier you will find it.

KNITTING

Blocking

So you have finished all the pieces - well done! Blocking is a method used to smooth out your work and set the shapes of your pieces. You basically shape it, wet it, and then leave it to dry. This allows the yarn fibres to relax and will create a more relaxed, fluid finish. It can also even out the size of your pieces and so, with the help of your tension swatch, you can ensure all the parts of your project are the size that they need to be.

The two main blocking methods I use are steam blocking and spray blocking. You can buy a lot of tools for blocking or just make do with what you have at home. The main tools are:

Blocking pins: These are T-shaped pins designed to hold the piece in place, but you can use long dressmaking pins that do NOT have a plastic head (they may melt when steamed or pressed with an iron).

Blocking wires: These are flexible wires that can be woven into pieces to help block curves on the sides of a project. Wires are particularly useful for blocking lace and finer yarns.

Blocking board: These have a grid on them, like graph paper, so you can easily measure your pieces and make sure they are straight. If you do not have a blocking board, you can use a padded surface like a large piece of foam or a folded towel. One great idea is to make your own blocking board. Simply get an MDF board and cover it with a layer of wadding and gingham fabric pulled tight and stapled to it.

Tape measure or ruler: If you need to block a piece to specific dimensions stated in a pattern, then you'll need a tape measure or ruler to ensure you block each piece to the correct size.

Steam iron: An electric iron that generates a good amount of hot steam is invaluable for blocking knitted and crocheted pieces. But always take good care when steaming a piece and make sure that you don't scald yourself.

Spray bottle: A basic spray bottle that you can pick up at a hardware store or gardening centre can be used to mist an item as an alternative to steaming.

Knitting Essentials

Pinning out a piece for blocking

Take time when shaping and pinning out any piece as once it has been steamed or sprayed, any irregularities in the shaping will become 'set' as it dries. For a garment, pin the centre length and then width, followed by the corners. Use as many pins as you need to make it smooth or use special blocking wires to create smooth edges. All pins or wires will come with instructions on how to get the best results.

Lay out the knitted piece right side down on the blocking board or surface. Use the printed grid or checked pattern of the gingham fabric to make sure that any edges that are supposed to be straight are straight.

Using a tape measure or ruler, ease the piece to the correct dimensions given in the pattern instructions.

Using blocking pins or dressmaking pins, pin the piece out, sliding the pins through the edge stitches of the piece and into the board or wadding. Start by pinning out the corners and then work around the edges between pinned corners. Use lots and lots of pins, placing them around 1cm (½ inch) apart, to make sure the edges are smooth.

Take care to make sure that the piece is symmetrical, if necessary. If blocking any piece that has a knitted rib, do not stretch the ribbing as it may lose its elasticity.

Blocking methods

I prefer to block a piece by either spray or steam blocking. You can wet block, where the piece is fully submerged in lukewarm water, but that method is not suitable for all fibres and I find that the piece then takes ages to dry. With wet blocking, a fabric can sometimes stretch and grow in size, or even felt slightly. Check the ball band to see if the manufacturer gives any advice on the best method to use for blocking. Go lightly when blocking as pressing too firmly may flatten a delicate stitch pattern or cable, losing its three-dimensionality, or the fabric could go limp.

Steam blocking

This method is my preferred way to block items.

- Hold a steam iron or a steamer above your item, hovering a few centimetres (an inch) away from the surface, so the steam penetrates the fibres. Do not allow the plate of the iron to touch the piece.

- Now the fibres have relaxed, you can manipulate them further into shape, if you need to.

- After steaming, leave your garment to rest and dry thoroughly before unpinning.

Spray blocking

This method is best for delicate fibres.

- Use a specially designed flattening spray or fill a clean spray bottle with wool wash (I like to do this so my knitting smells nice, rather than like a soggy sheep!). Or you can just use room temperature water.

- Spritz the knitted fabric with a fine mist. You don't need to saturate the fabric, you just need to dampen it with enough moisture to make some steam.

- Hover the hot iron (with the steam function turned off) over the piece to turn the moisture from the spray that is now within the knitted fibres into steam.

- Re-adjust the shape of your piece. Spray any dry sections as you reshape it.

- Leave your project to dry thoroughly before unpinning; this may take a day or two.

Sewing in yarn ends

When you have finished knitting your pieces, you will be left with yarn ends that need sewing in. I hate this bit, but you have to do it to neaten your pieces up. After all your knitting efforts, it is worthwhile. There are no hard and fast rules about weaving or sewing in yarn ends, but it is important that they are secure and not visible from the right side of your piece.

Sewing in yarn ends on cast-on and cast-off (bound-off) edges

Leave your cast-on and cast-off (bound-off) yarn ends as long as possible, then use these ends for sewing up seams. Any other yarn ends need to be discreetly hidden within the knitted fabric. Sew any seams before tackling the remaining yarn ends not being seamed that need to be woven in.

One: Using a blunt-tipped sewing needle, take the tip under a few stitches along the edge of the piece. Turn, then take it back again in the opposite direction. Trim the yarn end back, so it's all neat and tidy.

Sewing in yarn ends on stripes or intarsia

In intarsia and colourwork pieces, you will be left with yarn ends not just at the start and finish of your piece but throughout your work. When sewing in yarn ends, you need to weave the yarn ends on the same colour stitches.

One: Using a blunt-tipped sewing needle, take the tip through the purl bumps of a few stitches across the WS of the piece, following the row along the colour join.

Two: Turn, then take it back again in the opposite direction. Trim the yarn end to neaten. Weave each yarn end into stitches of its own colour and make sure all the stitches lie flat.

Sewing seams →

As I have knitted more and more, I've found that different ways of sewing up suit various garments depending on the edge and angle I am working at. I always try to use the yarn I am working with, providing it is strong enough, to sew the seams unless the pattern calls for another type of yarn or thread. Whatever you use to sew the seams, make sure it can be laundered in the same way as the yarn.

KNITTING

Sewing seams with mattress stitch

Mattress stitch joins the side edges of your knitted stocking (stockinette) stitch pieces with a neat, virtually invisible seam. It is also used when working in rib stitch and it is ideal for sewing up hats and sweaters. I like it because it is worked from the right side and so as you stitch up, you can see how the finished garment will look. You can work this stitch on garter stitch, but you alternate working into the top and bottom loops of the stitches. Taking a whole stitch into the seam is the neatest way of working mattress stitch, but if the yarn is bulky or if you need a slimmer seam then take half a stitch, although it won't be quite as invisible.

Sewing an invisible seam edge to edge

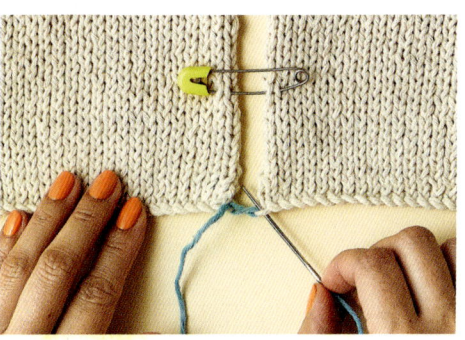

One: With RS facing up, line the items up next to each other. Thread a blunt-tipped sewing needle with your yarn and pass up through the RH piece and down through the LH piece, like a figure of eight, so the yarn comes from the back of the RH piece between the first and second edge stitches.

Two: Working from the front, take the needle across to the opposing left-hand piece and take it under the horizontal bar between the first and second stitches and bring the yarn underneath.

Three: Take the needle across again to the right-hand piece and take it under the next two horizontal bars between the first and second stitches. If the pieces are big you might want to stabilize them with safety pins, so they do not slip around.

Four: Continue to the end, alternating between the left and right sides, taking the needle under two bars at a time, adjusting the tension as you go. When you have worked a few centimetres (an inch), gently pull the yarn taut to close the seam. As you close the seam, the edge stitches of each piece turn to the back of the work, leaving a slight ridge.

Knitting Essentials

Sewing an invisible horizontal seam

This is another way to make an invisible seam, but this time it is used to join the cast-on and cast-off (bound-off) edges of knitted pieces.

One: Line up the two edges horizontally, with the right sides facing upwards. Insert the needle under the first stitch on the right, just above the cast-on edge.

Two: Take the needle back down under the corresponding stitch on the cast-off (bound-off) edge.

Three: Insert the needle under the next stitch to the left on the top edge, then back down again. Your yarn will form a line of 'V' shapes.

Four: Continue to the end to complete the seam. Pull the yarn taut as you work to conceal the cast-on and cast-off (bound-off) edges, which will turn to the back of the work.

Sewing an invisible vertical–horizontal seam

If you are attaching a vertical edge to a horizontal edge, such as the top of a sleeve to an arm, it is a similar technique to the invisible horizontal seam.

One: Line up the pieces. Insert the needle under a stitch of the bound-off edge of the vertical item, then insert it under one horizontal bar between the first and second stitch of the horizontal piece.

Two: On the vertical piece, insert the needle down through the centre of the next stitch and then up through the centre of the adjacent stitch.

Three: If there are more stitches in the vertical piece, occasionally pick up two horizontal bars on the horizontal piece and then under the corresponding stitch on the other side.

Four: Continue to the end to complete the seam. Pull the yarn taut as you work to conceal the edges of each piece.

Knitted Accesso

EASY

Ribbed Dickie

A dickie is like a neck and chest warmer to wear under a jacket or coat for warmth and cosiness. It is slightly shaped at the front to sit flat over the chest. This pattern uses a super-chunky yarn, so it is quick to knit up. This dickie is ideal for adding a pop of seasonal colour to liven up an old coat but does not add any bulk or weight.

Measurements
One size
Approx. 34cm (13½ in) wide
Approx. 21cm (8¼ in) from shoulder to hem and 32cm (12½ in) overall from neck edge to hem

What you will need
- Rowan Big Wool
  100% merino wool
  80m (87 yards) per 100g (3½ oz)

Quantity:

One-colour version
- 2 x 100g (3½ oz) balls in Citron (091)

Three-colour stripe version
- **A** 1 x 100g (3½ oz) ball in Midori (093)
- **B** 1 x 100g (3½ oz) ball in Steel Blue (052)
- **C** 1 x 100g (3½ oz) ball in Oasis (092)

- 1 pair of 10mm (US 15) needles
- 10mm (US 15) circular needle, 40cm (16 in) length
- Stitch holders
- Stitch marker
- Yarn needle

Tension (gauge)
11 sts and 12 rows to 10cm (4 in) over 1x1 rib using 10mm (US 15) needles. Change the needle size as necessary to achieve the correct tension (gauge).

Abbreviations
See page 61.

Special technique
Short-row shaping (see pages 90–91).

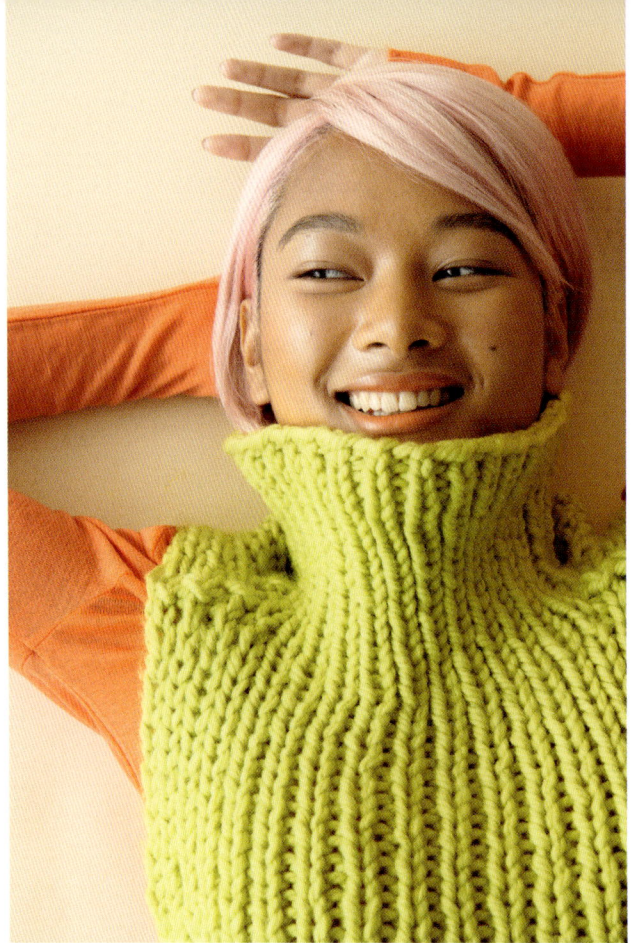

To make one-colour version

Back

Using 10mm (US 15) needles, cast on 37 sts and work in rib as follows:
Next row (RS): *P1, k1, rep from * to last st, p1.
Next row (WS): *K1, p1, rep from * to last st, k1.
Repeat last 2 rows 10 times more to complete 22 rows in total.

Shape shoulders
Next row (RS): Rib as set to last 4 sts, wrap next st and turn.
Next row (WS): Rib as set to last 4 sts, wrap next st and turn.
Next row: Rib 4 sts as set, turn.
Next row: Rib across all sts, picking up the wrap as you work.
Cut yarn leaving a long end.
Slip 8 sts onto a stitch holder for shoulder.
With RS of work facing, slip centre 21 sts onto a stitch holder.
Rejoin yarn to rem 8 sts and rib across all sts, picking up the wrap as you work.
Cut yarn leaving a long end.
Slip 8 sts onto a stitch holder for shoulder.

Front

Using 10mm (US 15) needles, cast on 33 sts and work in rib as follows:
Next row (RS): *P1, k1, rep from * to last st, p1.
Next row: *K1, p1, rep from * to last st, k1.
Next row (inc): (P1, k1) twice, p1, m1, rib as set to last 5 sts, m1, (p1, k1) twice, p1. *35 sts.*
Next row: (K1, p1) twice, k2, *p1, k1, rep from * to last 5 sts, (k1, p1) twice, k1.
Next row: (P1, k1) twice, p2, *k1, p1, rep from * to last 5 sts, (p1, k1] twice, p1.
Next row: (K1, p1) twice, k2, *p1, k1, rep from * to last 5 sts, (k1, p1) twice, k1.
Next row (inc): (P1, k1) twice, p1, m1, *p1, k1, rep from * to last 6 sts, p1, m1, (p1, k1) twice, p1. *37 sts.*
Next row: *K1, p1, rep from * to last st, k1.
Next row: *P1, k1, rep from * to last st, p1.
Next row: *K1, p1, rep from * to last st, k1.
Repeat last 2 rows 6 times more to complete 22 rows in total.

Shape shoulders
Next row: Rib as set to last 4 sts, wrap next st and turn
Next row: Rib as set to last 4 sts, wrap next st and turn.
Next row: Rib 4 sts as set, turn.
Next row: Rib across all sts, picking up the wrap as you work.
Cut yarn leaving a long end.
Slip 8 sts onto a stitch holder for shoulder.
With RS of work facing, slip centre 21 sts onto a stitch holder.
Rejoin yarn to rem 8 sts and rib across all sts picking up the wrap as you work.
Cut yarn leaving a long end.
Slip 8 sts onto a stitch holder for shoulder.

Join both shoulders using the three-needle cast off (bind off) method with wrong sides tog so that the seam is on the outside of your work and work the sts in rib.

Neck

With RS facing, using 10mm (US 15) circular needle and beg at the left shoulder, pick up and knit 2 sts down left front neck, rib as set across 21 sts from centre front stitch holder, pick up and knit 2 sts up right front neck, 3 sts down right back neck, rib as set across 21 sts from centre back stitch holder and pick up and knit 3 sts up left back neck, place marker to show start of round. *52 sts*.
Work in rib as follows, slipping marker as you work:
Next round: *P1, k1, rep from * to end of round.
Repeat last round 15 times more.
Cast off (bind off) in rib.

To finish

Weave in any yarn ends.

To make stripe version

Work the same as the one-colour version but use the following stripe sequence:
8 rows **A**
8 rows **B**
8 rows **C**
8 rows **A**
8 rows **B**

Finish the final 2 rows of the shoulder shaping using **C**.
Use **A** to pick up the sts for neck and work 7 more rows in rib using **A**.
Finish the neck with 8 rows **B** and cast off (bind off) using **B**.

Masterclass

Short-row shaping

This technique involves turning the work before the row is completed, hence the term "short rows". The result is that one part of the work has more rows than the rest, creating shaping for elements such as heels or collars.

Wrapping and turning on a knit row

If you just turn on a short row, a hole will appear between the stitches worked and not worked. This can be fixed by "wrapping" a slipped stitch at the point where the work is turned. When all the short rows are complete, you then work across the entire row of stitches, and pick up the wraps around the slipped stitches to hide them, so that each hole is still closed but the wrap has disappeared. Depending on how many short rows the pattern asks you to make, there may be several wraps to pick up in one row.

One   Knit to the position of the turn. Slip the next stitch purlwise from the lefthand needle to the righthand needle.

Two   Bring the yarn forward between the points of the needles.

Three   Slip the stitch back onto the lefthand needle.

Four   Take the yarn to the back, ready to purl the next row, and turn the work.

Picking up the wrap on a knit row

One To hide the wrap, knit to the wrapped stitch. Insert the righthand needle up through the front of the wrap.

Two Keeping the wrap on the righthand needle, insert the needle into the stitch and knit the wrap and the stitch together as one stitch.

Picking up the wrap on a purl row

One To hide then wrap, purl to the wrapped stitch. Insert the righthand needle up through the back of the wrap.

Two Keeping the wrap on the righthand needle, insert the needle into the stitch and purl the wrap and the stitch together as one stitch.

Knitted Accessories

EASY

Leg Warmers

Fun and retro accessories, made using trendy mohair yarn in modern pastel colours, these leg warmers are knitted on circular needles to be seam-free for comfort and in stretchy rib for a good fit. A great beginner's project for learning to work in the round, I think these also make a fabulous gift or for heading out to the roller disco!!

Measurements
One size
Approx. 22cm (8¾ in) around and 40cm (16 in) long

What you will need
- Debbie Bliss Nell
  78% mohair, 13% merino wool, 9% polyamide
  100m (109 yards) per 50g (1¾ oz)

Quantity:
- **A** 1 x 50g (1¾ oz) ball in Lilac (05)
- **B** 1 x 50g (1¾ oz) ball in Rose (09)
- **C** 1 x 50g (1¾ oz) ball in Aqua (06)
- **D** 1 x 50g (1¾ oz) ball in Jade (07)
- 6mm (US 10) circular knitting needle, 40cm (16 in) length, or double-pointed needles
- Stitch marker
- Yarn needle

Tension (gauge)
22 sts and 17 rows to 10cm (4 in) over 2x2 rib on 6mm (US 10) needles. Change needle size as necessary to achieve correct tension (gauge).

Abbreviations
See page 61.

Special technique
Working in the round (see pages 100–101).

Note: Avoiding a colour jog
When working in the round and knitting different colour stripes, there will always be a "jog" in each new colour at the start of the round. To disguise this, work the first round in the new colour yarn, leaving the tail of the new colour at the WS of the work for sewing in later. When you reach the start of the second round, slip the righthand needle purlwise into the stitch below the first stitch in the new colour and lift it onto the lefthand needle. Knit the lifted stitch and first stitch of the last round together in the new colour.

Stripe sequence

12 rounds **A**
4 rounds **B**
2 rounds **A**
8 rounds **C**
6 rounds **D**
6 rounds **A**
2 rounds **C**
4 rounds **B**
2 rounds **D**
4 rounds **B**
2 rounds **A**
6 rounds **D**
2 rounds **A**
8 rounds **C**

To make

(Make two the same)
Using 6mm (US 10) circular needles or double-pointed needles and **A**, cast on 44 sts.
Place marker to show start of round and join to work in the round, taking care not to twist the stitches.
Round 1: *K2, p2, rep from * to end of round.
Rep Round 1, following stripe sequence as given, until work meas 40cm (16 in) from cast-on edge.
Cast off (bind off) in rib as set.

To finish

Weave in any yarn ends.

Balaclava

EASY

This super-trendy accessory keeps your head, ears, and neck warm during winter or on the ski slopes. Pull it down over your face for maximum warmth or fold it up to form a hat when going indoors. A great beginner's project to learn simple colour change and shaping for the crown, as well as casting stitches on and off in the middle of a row for the front opening. You'll soon be making them for all your friends.

Measurements
One size
Approx. 38cm (15 in) long

What you will need
- Rowan Pure Wool Superwash Worsted
  100% wool
  200m (218 yards) per 100g (3½ oz)

Quantity:
- **A** 1 x 100g (3½ oz) ball in Periwinkle (146)
- **B** 1 x 100g (3½ oz) ball in Tiger (201)
- 4mm (US 6) circular needle, 40cm (16 in) length
- Set of four 4mm (US 6) double-pointed needles
- Stitch marker
- Yarn needle

Tension (gauge)
33 sts and 28 rows to 10cm (4 in) over rib using 4mm (US 6) needles. Change needle size as necessary to achieve correct tension (gauge).

Abbreviations
See page 61.

Special technique
Working in the round (see pages 100–101).

Knitted Accessories

To make

Using 4mm (US 6) circular needle and **A**, cast on 108 sts, place marker to show start of round and work in the round as follows, making sure that stitches are not twisted when you start working:
Rib round: *K2, p2, rep from * to end of round.
Repeat last round 27 times more, ending at marker.
Change to **B** and work a further 36 rounds in rib as set, ending at marker.

Make front opening

Next round: Rib 38 sts as set, cast off (bind off) next 34 sts in patt, rib as set to end of round.
Next round: Rib as set, casting on 34 sts over the cast-off (bound-off) sts of previous round, rib as set to end of round.
Work a further 22 rounds in rib as set, ending at marker.

Shape crown

Once knitting becomes too tight for the circular needle, transfer the work evenly onto three double-pointed needles and knit with the fourth needle.
Round 1: *K2, p2tog, (k2, p2) twice, rep from * to end of round. *99 sts*.
Rounds 2 and 3: *K2, p1, (k2, p2) twice, rep from * to end of round.
Round 4: *K1, ssk, (k2, p2) twice, rep from * to end of round. *90 sts*.
Rounds 5 and 6: *K4, p2, k2, p2, rep from * to end of round.
Round 7: *K1, k2tog, k1, p2, k2, p2, rep from * to end of round. *81 sts*.
Rounds 8 and 9: *K3, p2, k2, p2, rep from * to end of round.
Round 10: *K1, k2tog, p2, k2, p2, rep from * to end of round. *72 sts*.
Rounds 11 and 12: *K2, p2, rep from * to end of round.
Round 13: *K2tog, p2, k2, p2, rep from * to end of round. *63 sts*.
Rounds 14 and 15: *K1, p2, k2, p2, rep from * to end of round.
Round 16: *K1, p2tog, k2, p2tog, rep from * to end of round. *45 sts*.
Round 17: *K1, p1, k2tog, p1, rep from * to end of round. *36 sts*.

To finish

Cut working yarn leaving long end. Thread yarn through rem sts, sliding them off the needles, pull up tightly and fasten off securely.
Weave in any yarn ends.

Masterclass

Working in the round

Working in the round, or circular knitting as it is also known, can be a quick way of knitting as you are always working on the right side and you don't have any side seams to sew once you've finished.

Knitting on circular needles

One — Circular needles, where two short needles are connected by a flexible cable, are also good for making heavier projects, like a throw, as the weight of the knitted fabric can rest on your lap on the connecting cable.

Two — Using your preferred cast-on method, cast on the number of stitches needed on to one of the points of the short needles just as you would if using regular needles. Spread out the cast-on stitches evenly along the length of the cable between the two points, but without stretching them. Before you join the stitches into a round, it is crucial to check the cast-on edge is not twisted.

Three — Slip the first stitch from the lefthand needle onto the righthand needle in order to close the gap between the first and last cast-on stitches.

Four — Lift the last stitch on the righthand needle over the stitch just slipped from the lefthand needle without dropping either stitch – you are simply reversing the positions of the stitches.

Five — The first stitch in the first round is the beginning of the round – all subsequent rounds start in the same position, unless instructed otherwise. Place a stitch marker on the needle at the start of the first round before knitting the first stitch.

Knit the stitches from the lefthand needle point onto the righthand needle point, sliding them along the connecting cable as you work. When you get back to the stitch marker, you have completed one round. Slip the stitch marker onto the righthand needle point, ready to knit the next round.

Knitted Accessories

EASY

Odd Socks

Socks are one of the first projects that come to mind when people take up knitting, but they aren't always the easiest. This is a starter pattern and the only sock pattern that you'll need. Making a matching pair can be boring, so these are deliberately mis-matched with neon colours to stand out from the crowd. Designed with rib for stretch across the top, a denser rib for a reinforced heel, and stocking stitch for comfort on the sole, these socks are made using a special sock yarn.

Measurements

Adult size	S	M	L	
Foot circumference	20	23	25	cm
	8	9	10	in

What you will need
- Coop Knits Socks Yeah!
  75% fine superwash merino wool, 25% nylon
  212m (231 yards) per 50g (1¾ oz)

Quantity:
- **A** 1 x 50g (1¾ oz) hank in Chryso (108)
- **B** 1 x 50g (1¾ oz) hank in Helium (1001)
- **C** 1 x 50g (1¾ oz) hank in Melanite (121)
- **D** 1 x 50g (1¾ oz) hank in Xenon (1004)
- 2.5mm (US 1–2) circular knitting needle or double-pointed needles
- Stitch marker (optional)
- Stitch holders
- Yarn needle

Tension (gauge)
36 sts and 50 rows to 10cm (4 in) over St st on 2.5mm (US 1–2) needles. Change needle size as necessary to achieve correct tension (gauge).

Abbreviations
See page 61.

Special techniques
Working in the round (see pages 100–101).
Grafting stitches together (see page 107).

To make

First sock

Cuff and leg
Using **A**, cast on 64[72:80] sts. Join to work in the round. Place beg of round marker.
Round 1: * K1, p1, rep from * to end of round.
This round sets 1x1 rib.
Work a 7 rounds more in 1x1 rib.
Change to **B**.
Next round: Knit.
Work 22 rounds in 1x1 rib.
Change to **D**.
Next round: Knit.
Next round: * P2, K2, rep from * to end of round.
This round sets 2x2 rib.
Work 19 rounds more in 2x2 rib.
Change to **C**.
Next round: Knit.
Work 8 rounds in 2x2 rib.
Change to **A**.
Next round: Knit.
Work 8 rounds in 2x2 rib.

Heel flap
Next round: Using **A** patt 30[34:38], using **B**, knit across rem 34[38:42] sts.
Turn work so WS is facing. Work heel flap back and forth on next 34[38:42] sts. Keep rem 30[34:38] sts on stitch holder for instep.
Row 1 (WS): Sl1p, purl to end.
Row 2: (Sl1k, k1) 17[19:21] times.
Rep these 2 rows a further 13[14:15] times, then Row 1 once more.

Heel turn
Change to **A**.
Row 1 (RS): Sl1k, k20[22:24], ssk, k1, turn, leave rem sts unworked.
Row 2: Sl1p, p9, p2tog, p1, turn, leave rem sts unworked.
Row 3: Sl1k, knit to 1 st before gap, ssk, k1, turn.
Row 4: Sl1p, purl to 1 st before gap, p2tog, p1, turn.
Rep these 2 rows until all heel sts have been worked. *22[24:26] sts rem.*

Gusset
Now working in the round once more continue as follows:
Set-up round: Sl1k, k21[23:25], pick up 15[16:17] sts along edge of heel (this is one stitch from every slipped stitch), rib 30[34:38] sts, pick up 15[16:17] sts down edge of heel, k37[40:43]. You are now at the start of the sock upper.
Place beg of round marker. *82[90:100] sts.*
Round 1: Rib 30[34:38], ssk, k to last 2 sts, k2tog. *2 sts dec.*
Round 2: Rib 30[34:38], k to end of round.
These 2 rounds set gusset shaping.
Dec as set until 64[72:80] sts rem.
Work 8 rounds in patt as set.
Change to **D**.
Next round: Knit.
Work 16 rounds in pattern.
Change to **C**.
Next round: Knit.
Cont in pattern until work meas 6[6:7]cm (2¼[2¼:2¾] in) less than desired foot length.
Change to **B**.
Next round: Knit.
Pattern 2 rounds.

Shape toe
Change to **A**.
Next round: (K1, ssk, k26[30:34], k2tog, k1) twice. *4 sts dec. 60[68:76] sts.*
Next round: Knit.
Next round: (K1, ssk, k24[28:32], k2tog, k1) twice. *4 sts dec. 56[64:72] sts.*
Next round: Knit.
Working 2 sts less between decreases continue in this way until 20[24:24] sts rem.

To finish

Cut yarn leaving a 30cm (12 in) end.
Join toe sts using the grafting technique (see page 107).
Weave in any yarn ends, sewing them into the sock upper rather than the sole as this part of the sock gets less wear.

Second sock

Cuff and leg
Using **D** cast on 64[72:80] sts. Join to work in the round. Place beg of round marker.
Round 1: *K1, p1, rep from * to end of round.
This round sets 1x1 rib.
Work 11 rounds more in 1x1 rib.
Change to **C**.
Next round: Knit.
Work 6 rounds in 1x1 rib.
Change to **D**.
Next round: Knit.
Work 11 rounds in 1x1 rib.
Change to **B**.
Next round: Knit.
Next round: *P2, k2, rep from * to end of round.
This round sets 2x2 rib.
Work a 18 rounds more in 2x2 rib.
Change to **D**.
Next round: Knit.
Work 9 rounds in 2x2 rib.
Change to **A**.
Next round: Knit.
Work 8 rounds in 2x2 rib.

Heel flap
Next round: Using **A**, patt 30[34:38], using **C** knit across rem 34[38:42] sts.
Turn work so WS is facing. Work heel flap back and forth on next 34[38:42] sts. Keep rem 30[34:38] sts on stitch holder for instep.
Row 1 (WS): Sl1p, purl to end.
Row 2: (Sl1k, k1) 17[19:21] times.
Rep these 2 rows a further 13[14:15] times, then Row 1 once more.

Heel turn
Change to **A**.
Row 1 (RS): Sl1k, k20[22:24], ssk, k1, turn, leave rem sts unworked.
Row 2: Sl1p, p9, p2tog, p1, turn, leave rem sts unworked.
Row 3: Sl1k, knit to 1 st before gap, ssk, k1, turn.
Row 4: Sl1p, purl to 1 st before gap, p2tog, p1, turn.
Repeat these 2 rows until all heel sts have been worked. *22[24:26] sts rem.*

Gusset
Now working in the round once more continue as follows:
Set up round: Sl1k, k21[23:25], pick up 15[16:17] sts along edge of heel (this is one stitch from every slipped stitch), rib 30[34:38] sts, pick up 15[16:17] sts down edge of heel, k37[40:43]. You are now at the start of the sock upper.
Place beg of round marker. *82[90:98] sts.*
Round 1: Rib 30[34:38], ssk, knit to last 2 sts, k2tog. *2 sts dec.*
Round 2: Rib 30[34:38], knit to end of round.
These 2 rounds set gusset shaping.
Dec as set until 64[72:80] sts rem.
Work 5 rounds as set.
Change to **B**.
Next round: Knit.
Continue for 30 rounds in pattern for 7cm (2¾ in).
Change to **A**.
Next round: Knit.
Continue in pattern until work meas 6[6:7]cm (2¼[2¼:2¾] in) less than desired foot length.
Change to **D**.
Next round: Knit.
Pattern 2 rounds.

Shape toe
Change to **B**.
Next round: (K1, ssk, k26[30:34], k2tog, k1) twice. *4 sts dec. 60[68:76] sts.*
Next round: Knit.
Next round: (K1, ssk, k24[28:32], k2tog, k1) twice. *4 sts dec. 56[64:72] sts.*
Next round: Knit.
Working 2 sts less between decreases continue in this way until 20[24:24] sts rem.

To finish

Cut yarn leaving a 30cm (12 in) end.
Join toe sts using the grafting technique (see masterclass opposite).
Weave in any yarn ends, sewing them into the sock upper rather than the sole as this part of the sock gets less wear.

Knitted Accessories

Masterclass

Grafting stitches together

Grafting two separate pieces together into one seamless creation can be neatly done using this particular technique, which gives for a super-tidy finish. This can be used in items where you do not want to feel a seam, such as the toe of a sock.

One — With the same number of stitches on both needles, place the needles parallel, with the RS of the work facing upwards. Cut the working yarn from the back piece leaving a long tail around four times the length of the edge to be grafted. Thread a yarn large-eyed sewing with the yarn tail. To start, bring the needle from the back to the front piece and pass it through the first stitch of the front piece as if to purl. Pull the yarn through, leaving the stitch on the needle. From the back again, bring the needle through the first stitch of the back piece as if to knit and pull the yarn through, leaving the stitch on the needle. Take the needle through the first stitch of the front piece as if to knit and take it off the needle. Then, take the needle through the next stitch of the front piece as if to purl, leaving the stitch on the needle.

Two — Take the needle through the first stitch of the back piece as if to purl and take it off needle. Take the needle through the next stitch of the back piece as if to knit, leaving the stitch on the needle.

Three — Continue taking the needle through a stitch from the front and then through the next stitch from the back, alternating between the front and back pieces, until you have one stitch left on each needle. To complete the last two stitches, slip the front stitch knitwise and slip the back stitch purlwise. Take the yarn to the inside of your work.

Four — Adjust the sewn stitches as you make them so that they have the same tension as the knitted stitches. If the sewn stitches are uneven, you can use the sewing needle to ease the yarn along the row to even up the tension. Sew the yarn end into the wrong side of your knitting.

EASY

Long Scarf

A scarf was the first thing I ever knitted, and this is another brilliant beginner's project – a super-long scarf in pastel-bright block colours of chunky mohair yarn. Using a rib stitch adds texture, but also means that the scarf lays flat so the edges do not curl inwards, and that it is fully reversible. For a designer finish, fringe the scarf in blocks of colour – it's all in the detail!

Measurements
One size
Approx. 32cm (12½ in) wide and 210cm (82½ in) long

What you will need
- Debbie Bliss Nell
  78% mohair, 13% merino wool, 9% polyamide
  100m (109 yards) per 50g (1¾ oz)

Quantity:
- **A** 2 x 50g (1¾ oz) balls in Jade (07)
- **B** 2 x 50g (1¾ oz) balls in Heather (04)
- **C** 2 x 50g (1¾ oz) balls in Lilac (05)
- **D** 2 x 50g (1¾ oz) balls in Willow (08)
- **E** 1 x 50g (1¾ oz) ball in Rose (09)

- 1 pair 6mm (US 10) knitting needles
- 6mm (US J/10) crochet hook
- Yarn needle

Tension (gauge)
17 sts and 18 rows to 10cm (4 in) over 1x1 rib using 6mm (US 10) needles. Change needle size as necessary to achieve correct tension (gauge).

Abbreviations
See page 61.

Special technique
Adding fringing (see pages 180–181).

Note: Joining in new colours
On the row before you need introduce the new colour, work to the last stitch. Take the end of the new colour and use it together with the current yarn in work to complete the last stitch, creating a "double stitch". On the first stitch of the next row, work the double stitch as one stitch with just the new colour. This will securely anchor your new yarn and avoid creating any unsightly knots or bumps.

Knitted Accessories

Stripe sequence

8 rows **A**
4 rows **B**
42 rows **A**
28 rows **C**
8 rows **D**
24 rows **E**
4 rows **A**
12 rows **E**
8 rows **D**
24 rows **B**
24 rows **C**
8 rows **D**
8 rows **E**
36 rows **B**
8 rows **A**
4 rows **C**
24 rows **A**
2 rows **E**
14 rows **A**
36 rows **C**
28 rows **D**
8 rows **B**
16 rows **D**

To make

Using 6mm (US 10) needles and **A**, cast on 55 sts and work in rib as follows:
Row 1 (RS): P1, *k1, p1, rep from * to end.
Row 2: *K1, p1, rep from * to last st, k1.
Rep these 2 rows following stripe sequence as given.
Cast off (bind off) in rib.

To finish

Weave in any yarn ends neatly along the row, not up the sides of the scarf.

Fringing
Add a tassel (see masterclass on page 181) to every alternate stitch along both cast-on and cast-off (bound-off) edges to create an evenly spaced fringe. Use 35cm (14 in) lengths of yarn and follow the photographs as a colour guide. Trim the fringing to approx. 15cm (6 in), or to the length preferred.

Knitted
Garment

s

04

EASY

Fringe Sweater

Deceptively easy to knit, this cropped, boxy sweater looks fab on both you and your mini me! Made in rectangles of repeating moss stitch, in this pattern you will learn easy short-row shaping for the shoulders, creating a neater finish than stepped shoulders, and a three-needle cast off to provide a smart external seam. Have fun with adding fringing in coordinating or contrast colours, but don't get too carried away – sometimes less is more!

Measurements
See chart below for adult sizes and see chart on page 117 for junior sizes.

Materials
- Wool Couture Cheeky Chunky 100% merino wool 65m (71 yards) per 100g (3½ oz)

ADULT SIZE Quantity:
- 10[11:13:14:15] x 100g (3½ oz) balls in Mustard

JUNIOR SIZE Quantity:
- **A** 5[5:6] x 100g (3½ oz) balls in Natural Cream
- **B** scraps in Raspberry, for fringing
- **C** scraps in Aqua, for fringing
- **D** scraps in Lemon, for fringing
- **E** scraps in Aquamarine, for fringing
- 1 pair 12mm (US 17) knitting needles
- 10mm (US 15) circular needle, 60cm (24 in) length
- Stitch markers
- Stitch holders
- 8mm (US L/11) crochet hook
- Yarn needle

Tension (gauge)
9 sts and 12 rows to 10cm (4 in) over moss (seed) st on 12mm (US 17) needles. Change needle size to achieve correct tension (gauge).

Abbreviations
See page 61.

Special technique
Short-row shaping (see pages 90–91).

Adult size	XS	S	M	L/XL	XXL	
To fit chest	71–86	91.5–106.5	111.5–117	122–137	142–158	cm
	28–34	36–42	44–46	48–54	56–62	in
Actual chest	118	126.5	140	153.5	166.5	cm
	46½	49¾	55	60½	65½	in
Length	54	56	58	60	62	cm
	21¼	22	22¾	23½	24½	in
Sleeve length	36	36	36	36	36	cm
	14¼	14¼	14¼	14¼	14¼	in

Note: The first row is the right side of the work. To maintain moss (seed) st, if the st on lefthand needle presents as a knit stitch, work st as purl; if the st on lefthand needle presents as a purl stitch, work st as knit. Alternatively, attach a stitch marker to the right side of your work to keep track of it.

To make adult size

Back

Using 12mm (US 17) needles, cast on 55[59:65:71:77] sts.
Next row (RS): *K1, p1, rep from * to last st, k1.
Repeat last row for moss (seed) st until work meas 49[51:53:55:57]cm (19¼[20:20¾:21¾:22½] in) from cast-on edge, ending with RS facing for next row, placing markers at both sides when work meas 30[31:32:33:34]cm (11¾[12¼:12½:13:13½] in) from cast-on edge to show start of armholes.

Shape shoulders
Next row (RS): Patt to last 6[7:8:9:10] sts, wrap next st and turn.
Next row: Patt to last 6[7:8:9:10] sts, wrap next st and turn.
Next row: Patt to last 12[13:15:16:18] sts, wrap next st and turn.
Next row: Patt to last 12[13:15:16:18] sts, wrap next st and turn.
Next row: Patt 6[6:7:8:9] sts, turn.
Next row: Patt across all 18[19:22:24:27] sts, picking up wraps as you work.
Cut yarn leaving a long end.
Slip these 18[19:22:24:27] sts onto a stitch holder for shoulder.

With RS facing, slip centre 19[21:21:23:23] sts onto stitch holder for neckband.
Rejoin yarn to rem sts at neck edge and patt across all 18[19:22:24:27] sts, picking up wraps as you work.
Cut yarn leaving long end.
Slip these 18[19:22:24:27] sts onto a stitch holder for shoulder.

Front

Using 12mm (US 17) needles, cast on 55[59:65:71:77] sts.
Next row (RS): *K1, p1, rep from * to last st, k1.
Repeat last row for moss (seed) st until work meas 49[51:53:55:57]cm (19¼[20:20¾:21¾:22½] in) from cast-on edge, ending with RS facing for next row, placing markers at both sides when work meas 30[31:32:33:34]cm (11¾[12¼:12½:13:13½] in) from cast-on edge to show start of armholes.

Shape neck and shoulders
Next row (RS): Patt 23[24:27:29:32], turn and leave rem sts on stitch holder.
Next row: Cast off (bind off) 3 sts, patt to last 6[7:8:9:10] sts, wrap next st and turn.
Next row: Patt to end of row.
Next row: Cast off (bind off) 2 sts, patt to last 12[13:15:16:18] sts, wrap next st and turn.
Next row: Patt to end of row.
Next row: Patt across all 18[19:22:24:27] sts, picking up wraps as you work.
Cut yarn leaving a long end.
Slip these 18[19:22:24:27] sts onto stitch holder for shoulder.

With RS facing, slip centre 9[11:11:13:13] sts onto stitch holder.
Rejoin yarn to rem sts at neck edge and work as follows:
Next row (RS): Cast off (bind off) 3 sts, patt to last 6[7:8:9:10] sts, wrap next st and turn.
Next row: Patt to end of row.
Next row: Cast off (bind off) 2 sts, patt to last 12[13:15:16:18] sts, wrap next st and turn.
Next row: Patt to end of row.
Next row: Patt across all 18[19:22:24:27] sts, picking up wraps as you work.
Cut yarn leaving long end.
Slip these 18[19:22:24:27] sts onto stitch holder for shoulder.

Join both shoulders using the three-needle cast-off (bind-off) method with WS of work together so the external seam is on the outside of your work.

Sleeves (both alike)

With RS facing and using 12mm (US 17) needles, pick up and knit 35[37:39:41:43] sts evenly between armhole markers and work in moss (seed) st as follows:
Next row: *K1, p1, rep from * to last st, k1.
Repeat last row for moss (seed) st until sleeve meas 36cm (14¼ in) from pick-up.
Cast off (bind off) in moss (seed) st.

Neckband

With RS facing and using 10mm (US 17) circular needle, starting at left shoulder seam, pick up and knit 7 sts down left front neck, patt across 9[11:11:13:13] sts from holder, pick up and knit 7 sts up right front neck, 3 sts down right back neck, patt across 19[21:21:23:23] sts from holder and pick up and knit 3 sts up left back neck. Join to work in the round and place marker to show start of round. *48[52:52:56:56] sts.*
Next round: *K1, p1, rep from * to end of round.
Repeat this round for 1x1 rib until neckband meas 3.5cm (1½ in), ending at marker.
Cast off (bind off) in rib.

To finish

Weave in any yarn ends.
Join side and sleeve seams.

Fringing
Cut any leftover yarn into lengths of approx 33cm (13 in) long. For each fringe, take a length of yarn and fold in half. Push the crochet hook from back to front through the raised bump of a stitch. Using the crochet hook, pull the folded yarn down half-way through the stitch, then take the loop and pull the ends through to secure. Repeat in random patches across the front, back and sleeves, using the photograph as a guide. Trim each fringe to neaten to 15cm (6 in), or as preferred.

To make junior size

To fit age	2–3	4–5	6–7	years
Actual chest	64.5	73.5	82	cm
	25½	29	32¼	in
Length	33	35	37	cm
	13	13¾	14½	in
Sleeve length	17	17	17	cm
	6¾	6¾	6¾	in

Back

Using 12mm (US 17) needles and **A**, cast on 31[35:39] sts.
Next row (RS): *K1, p1, rep from * to last st, k1.
Repeat last row for moss (seed) st until work meas 28[30:32]cm (11[11¾:12½] in) from cast-on edge, ending with RS facing for next row, placing markers at both sides when work meas 16cm (6¼ in) from cast-on edge to show start of armholes.

Shape shoulders
Next row (RS): Patt to last 3[4:5] sts, wrap next st and turn.
Next row: Patt to last 3[4:5] sts, wrap next st and turn.
Next row: Patt to last 7[8:9] sts, wrap next st and turn.
Next row: Patt to last 7[8:9] sts, wrap next st and turn.
Next row: Patt 3[3:4] sts, turn.
Next row: Patt across all 10[11:13] sts, picking up wraps as you work.
Cut yarn leaving long end.
Slip these 10[11:13] sts onto stitch holder for shoulder.

With RS facing, slip centre 11[13:13] sts onto stitch holder for neckband.
Rejoin yarn to rem sts at neck edge and patt across all 10[11:13] sts, picking up wraps as you work.
Cut yarn leaving long end.
Slip these 10[11:13] sts onto stitch holder for shoulder.

Front

Using 12mm (US 17) needles, cast on 31[35:39] sts.
Next row (RS): *K1, p1, rep from * to last st, k1.
Repeat last row for moss (seed) st until work meas 28[30:32]cm (11[11¾:12½] in) from cast-on edge, ending with RS facing for next row, placing markers at both sides when work meas 16cm (6¼ in) from cast-on edge to show start of armholes.

Shape neck and shoulders
Next row (RS): Patt 14[15:17], turn and leave rem sts on stitch holder.
Next row: Cast off (bind off) 2 sts, patt to last 3[4:5] sts, wrap next st and turn.
Next row: Patt to end of row.
Next row: Cast off (bind off) 2 sts, patt to last 7[8:9] sts, wrap next st and turn.
Next row: Patt to end of row.
Next row: Patt across all 10[11:13] sts, picking up wraps as you work.
Cut yarn leaving long end.
Slip these 10[11:13] sts onto stitch holder for shoulder.

With RS facing, slip centre 3[5:5] sts onto stitch holder.
Rejoin yarn to rem sts at neck edge and work as follows:
Next row (RS): Cast off (bind off) 2 sts, patt to last 3[4:5] sts, wrap next st and turn.
Next row: Patt to end of row.
Next row: Cast off (bind off) 2 sts, patt to last 7[8:9] sts, wrap next st and turn.
Next row: Patt to end of row.
Next row: Patt across all 10[11:13] sts, picking up wraps as you work.
Cut yarn leaving long end.
Slip these 10[11:13] sts onto stitch holder for shoulder.

Join both shoulders using the three-needle cast-off (bind-off) method with WS of work together so the external seam is on the outside of your work.

Sleeves (both alike)

With RS facing and using 12mm (US 17) needles, pick up and knit 23[25:29] sts evenly between armhole markers and work in moss (seed) st as follows:
Next row: *K1, p1, rep from, * to last st, k1.
Rep last row until sleeve meas 17cm (6¾ in) from pick-up.
Cast off (bind off) in moss (seed) st.

Neckband

With RS facing, using 10mm (US 15) circular needle and **A**, starting at left shoulder seam, pick up and knit 6 sts down left front neck, patt across 3[5:5] sts from holder, pick up and knit 6 sts up right front neck, 3 sts down right back neck, patt across 11[13:13] sts from holder and pick up and knit 3 sts up left back neck. Join to work in the round and place marker to show start of round. *32[36:36] sts.*
Next round: *K1, p1, rep from * to end of round.
Repeat this round for 1x1 rib until neckband meas 2.5cm (1 in), ending at marker.
Cast off (bind off) in rib.

To finish

Weave in any yarn ends.
Join side and sleeve seams.

Fringing
Cut scraps of contrast colour yarns (**B, C, D, E**) into lengths of approx. 22cm (9 in) long. For each fringe, take a length of yarn and fold in half. Push the crochet hook from back to front through the raised bump of a stitch. Using the crochet hook pull the folded yarn down half-way through the stitch, then take the loop and pull the ends through to secure. Repeat in random patches of colour across the front, back and sleeves using the photograph as a guide. Trim each fringe to neaten to 10cm (4 in), or as preferred.

Cable Sweater

This sweater is a modern take on a traditional cable jumper, knitted in bold monochrome black and white with a slip stitch pattern to the front, back and sleeves and an oversized central cable. It is a great way to practise your cables (which are much easier to master than they appear!) and a stylish autumnal knit, ideal for layering up.

Measurements
See chart below. Suggested ease of 15cm (6 in) to 30cm (11¾ in).

Materials
- Cascade 220
  100% Peruvian highland wool
  200m (218 yards) per 100g (3½ oz)

Quantity:
- **A** 4[4:5:5:6:7] x 100g (3½ oz) balls in Black
- **B** 4[4:5:5:6:7] x 100g (3½ oz) balls in Natural
- 1 pair 5mm (US 8) knitting needles
- 1 pair 5.5mm (US 9) knitting needles
- 4.5mm (US 7) circular needle, 40cm (16 in) length
- 5mm (US 8) cable needle
- Stitch markers
- Stitch holders
- Yarn needle

Tension (gauge)
21 sts and 28 rows to 10cm (4 in) over two-colour rib on 5.5mm (US 9) needles. Change needle size as necessary to achieve correct tension (gauge).

Abbreviations
See pages 61 and 122.

Special techniques
Working cables (see page 125).
Working intarsia (see page 149).
Short-row shaping (see pages 90–91).

Note
The front is knitted using the intarsia colourwork method.

Adult size	XS	S/M	L/XL	XXL	XXXL	XXXXL	
Actual chest	109.5	121	132.5	144	161	172.5	cm
	43	47¾	52¼	56¾	63½	68	in
Length	61	63	65	67	69	71	cm
	24	24¾	25½	26½	27¼	28	in
Sleeve length	48	49	49	49	50	50	cm
	19	19¼	19¼	19¼	19¾	19¾	in

Special abbreviations

C10B (cable 10 back): Slip next 5 sts onto cable needle and hold at back of work, knit next 5 sts from left-hand needle, then knit 5 sts from cable needle.

C10F (cable 10 front): Slip next 5 sts onto cable needle and hold at front of work, knit next 5 sts from left-hand needle, then knit 5 sts from cable needle.

1x1 rib
Row 1 (RS): *K1, p1, rep from * to end of row.
Row 2: *K1, p1, rep from * to end of row.

2 colour rib pattern
Row 1 (RS): Using **B**, *p3, k1, slip 1 st purlwise, k1, rep from * to last 3 sts, p3.
Row 2: Using **B**, k3, *p3, k3, rep from * to end of row.
Row 3: Using **A**, *p3, yb, slip next 3 sts purlwise, yfwd, rep from * to last 3 sts, p3.
Row 4: Using **A**, k3, *yfwd, slip 1 st purlwise, p1, slip 1 st purlwise, yb, k3, rep from * to end of row.

Cable pattern worked over 20 sts
Row 1 (RS): Knit.
Row 2: Purl.
Row 3: Knit.
Row 4: Purl.
Row 5: C10B, C10F.
Row 6: Purl.
Row 7: Knit.
Row 8: Purl.
Row 9: Knit.
Row 10: Purl.
Row 11: Knit.
Row 12: Purl.
Rep these 12 rows.

To make

Back

Using 5mm (US 8) needles and **A**, cast on 108[122:132:146:162:178] sts and work 15 rows in 1x1 rib.
Next row (WS inc): Rib 10[16:14:19:17:29], m1, (rib 11[15:13:18:16:30], m1) 8[6:8:6:8:4] times, rib to end. *117[129:141:153:171:183] sts.*
Change to 5.5mm (US 9) needles.
Work in **2 colour rib pattern** as above until work meas 60[62:64:66:68:70]cm (23½[24½:25¼:26:26¾:27½] in) from cast-on edge, ending with RS facing for next row, placing markers at both sides when work meas 37[38:39:40:41:42]cm (14½[15:15¼:15¾:16¼:16½] in) from cast-on to show start of armholes.

Shape shoulders
The shoulders are worked in short row shaping. You will have to strand the colour you are not using over a few stitches so that it is in the right place for keeping the pattern correct.
Keeping pattern correct, work as follows:
Next row: Patt to last 8[11:12:14:16:18] sts, wrap next st and turn.
Next row: Patt to last 8[11:12:14:16:18] sts, wrap next st and turn.
Next row: Patt to last 16[21:24:28:33:36] sts, wrap next st and turn.
Next row: Patt to last 16[21:24:28:33:36] sts, wrap next st and turn.
Next row: Patt to last 25[31:36:42:50:55] sts, wrap next st and turn.
Next row: Patt to last 25[31:36:42:50:55] sts, wrap next st and turn.
Next row: Patt 10 sts, turn.
Next row: Patt across all 35[41:46:52:60:65] sts, picking up wraps as you work.
Cut yarn leaving a long end.
Slip these 35[41:46:52:60:65] sts onto a holder for shoulder.
With RS facing, slip centre 47[47:49:49:51:53] sts onto a holder.
Rejoin correct colour yarn to rem sts and patt to end of row picking up wraps as you work.
Cut yarn leaving a long end.
Slip these 35[41:46:52:60:65] sts onto a holder for shoulder.

Front

The front is worked in 2 colour rib with a centre cable panel worked in **A**. You will need to work the front using the intarsia

method so you will have to work with separate balls of yarn as follows:
1 ball **A** and 1 ball **B** for first 2 colour rib section, 1 ball **A** for centre cable section and 1 ball **A** and 1 ball **B** for second 2 colour rib section. You may find it easier to wind the yarn onto bobbins which stops them getting too tangled as you work. When working in intarsia always cross the yarn on the WS of your work to avoid holes.

Using 5mm (US 8) needles and **A**, cast on 108[122:132:146:162:178] sts and work 15 rows in 1x1 rib.
Next row (WS inc): (Rib 7[10:9:11:11:16], m1) 6[3:6:5:6:4] times, (rib 8[9:8:12:10:17], m1) 3[7:3:3:3:2] times, (rib 7[10:9:11:11:16], m1) 5[2:5:4:5:4] times, rib to end. *122[134:146:158:176:188] sts.*

Change to 5.5mm (US 9) needles and work row 1 of 2 colour rib and cable pattern as follows:
Next row (RS): P0[0:0:0:3:3] using **B**, work Row 1 of 2 colour rib using **B** on next 51[57:63:69:75:81] sts, place marker, work Row 1 of cable pattern using **A** over next 20 sts, place marker, work Row 1 of 2 colour rib using **B** on next 51[57:63:69:75:81] sts, p0[0:0:0:3:3] using **B**.
Beg with Row 2 of both patterns continue in patt until work meas 55[57:58:60:61:63] cm (21¾[22½:22¾:23½:24:24¾] in) from the cast-on edge, ending with RS facing for next row, and placing markers at both sides when work meas 37[38:39:40:41:42] cm (14½[15:15¼:15¾:16¼:16½] in) from cast-on edge to show start of armholes.

Shape neck
Next row (RS): Patt 48[54:59:65:73:78], turn leaving rem sts on stitch holder.
Next row: Cast off (bind off) 5 sts, patt to end of row. *43[49:54:60:68:73] sts.*
Next row: Patt to end of row.
Next row: Cast off (bind off) 3 sts, patt to end of row. *40[46:51:57:65:70] sts.*
Next row: Patt to last 3 sts, work 2 sts tog to dec, k1. *39[45:50:56:64:69] sts.*
Next row: P1, k2tog, patt as set to end of row. *38[44:49:55:63:68] sts.*
Next row: Patt to end of row.
Next row: P1, k2tog, patt as set to end of row. *37[43:48:54:62:67] sts.*
Next row: Patt to end of row.
Next row: P1, k2tog, patt as set to end of row. *36[42:47:53:61:66] sts.*
Next row: Patt to end of row.
Work until front meas same as back to shoulder shaping, ending with WS facing for next row.

Shape shoulders
The shoulders are worked in short row shaping. You will have to strand the colour not in use over a few stitches so that it is in the right place for keeping pattern correct.
Next row (WS): P1, k2tog, patt to last 8[11:12:14:16:18] sts, wrap next st and turn.
Next row: Patt to end of row.
Next row: Patt to last 16[21:24:28:33:36] sts, wrap next st and turn.
Next row: Patt to end of row.
Next row: Patt to last 25[31:36:42:50:55] sts, wrap next st and turn.
Next row: Patt 10, turn.
Next row: Patt across all 35[41:46:52:60:65] sts, picking up wraps as you work.
Cut yarn leaving a long end.
Slip these 35[41:46:52:60:65] sts onto a holder for shoulder.

With RS facing, slip centre 26[26:28:28:30:32] sts onto a holder. Rejoin correct colour yarn to rem sts and work as follows:
Next row (RS): Cast off (bind off) 5 sts, patt to end of row. *43[49:54:60:68:73] sts.*
Next row: Patt to end of row.
Next row: Cast off (bind off) 3 sts, patt to end of row. *40[46:51:57:65:70] sts.*
Next row: Patt to last 3 sts, work sts 2 tog to dec, p1. *39[45:50:56:64:69] sts.*
Next row: K1, k2tog, patt as set to end of row. *38[44:49:55:63:68] sts.*
Next row: Patt to end of row.
Next row: K1, k2tog, patt as set to end of row. *37[43:48:54:62:67] sts.*
Next row: Patt to end of row.
Next row: K1, k2tog, patt to end of row. *36[42:47:53:61:66] sts.*

Next row: Patt to end of row.
Work until front meas same as back to shoulder shaping, ending with RS facing for next row.

Shape shoulder

Next row (RS): K1, k2tog, patt to last 8[11:12:14:16:18] sts, wrap next st and turn.
Next row: Patt to end of row.
Next row: Patt to last 16[21:24:28:33:36] sts, wrap next st and turn.
Next row: Patt to end of row.
Next row: Patt to last 25[31:36:42:50:55] sts, wrap next st and turn.
Next row: Patt 10, turn.
Next row: Patt across all 35[41:46:52:60:65] sts, picking up wraps as you work.
Cut yarn leaving a long end.
Slip these 35[41:46:52:60:65] sts onto holder for shoulder.

Sleeves (both alike)

The sleeves are worked in 2 colour rib throughout.
Work increases as follows:
RS increase: P1, m1, patt to last st, m1, p1.
WS increase: K1, m1, patt to last st, m1, k1.

Work increases in Rev st st until you have enough sts to work another pattern repeat.

Using 5mm (US 8) needles and **A**, cast on 44[46:50:52:54:54] sts and work 15 rows in 1x1 rib.
Next row (WS inc): Rib 7[9:7:10:13:13], m1, (rib 5[7:6:8:14:14], m1) 6[4:6:4:2:2] times, rib to end of row. *51[51:57:57:57:57] sts.*
Change to 5.5mm (US 9) needles and work in 2 colour rib as above, inc 1 st at both ends of 3rd row and every following 5th[5th:5th:5th:5th:4th] row until 89[93:97:101:105:109] sts.
Cont straight in patt as set until sleeve meas 48[49:49:49:50:50] cm (19[19¼:19¼:19¼:19¾:19¾] in) from cast-on edge, ending with RS facing for next row. Cast off loosely.
Join both shoulders using **A** and three-needle cast off (bind off) method using k3, p3 rib with WS of work tog so seams are visible on outside of your work.

Neckband

With RS facing, 4.5mm (US 7) circular needle, **A**, and starting at left shoulder seam, pick up and knit 17 sts down left front neck, k26[26:28:28:30:32] sts from front holder, pick up and knit 17 sts up right front neck, 3 sts across right back neck, k47[47:49:49:51:53] sts from back holder and pick up and knit 4 sts across left back neck, place marker to show start of round. *114[114:118:118:122:126] sts.*
Next round: *K1, p1, rep from * to end of round.
Repeat last round for 1x1 rib until neckband meas 9cm (3½in), ending at marker.
Cast off (bind off) in rib.

To finish

Weave in any yarn ends.
With RS of work facing, pin and sew sleeves between armhole markers.
Join side and sleeve seams.

Masterclass

Working cables

Cabling is a traditional technique designed to add three-dimensional texture to knitting by moving a group of stitches across the fabric so the cable appears to travel over the piece. Usually worked in stocking (stockinette) stitch on a background of reverse stocking stitch for contrast, but other stitches can be used.

Cable back (cb)

Cable stitches are held at the back of the work on a short cable needle while the next stitches from the LH needle are worked. The stitches on the cable needle are then worked to create the "twist". A cable back creates a twist to the right. Any number of stitches can be used to make cables of varying thickness.

One   Work to the position of the cable as instructed in the pattern. Slip the specified number of stitches from the LH needle onto the cable needle (here it is five).

Two   Hold the cable needle and the stitches on it at the back of the work, then knit the next specified number of stitches from the LH needle. Now knit the stitches from the cable needle to complete the twist.

Cable front (cf)

Cable back and cable front are often used together to create a cable that snakes along the knitted fabric. A cable front is worked in the same way as a cable back, except the cable stitches are held at the front of the work. A cable front creates a twist to the left.

One   Work to the position of the cable as instructed in the pattern. Slip the specified number of stitches from the LH needle onto the cable needle (here it is five).

Two   Hold the cable needle and the stitches on it at the front of the work, then knit the next specified number of stitches from the LH needle. Now knit the stitches from the cable needle to complete the twist.

Knitted Garments

Top Down Fair Isle Sweater

This cosy Fair Isle sweater is a play on the traditional knits named after the colourwork technique originating from the Shetland Islands, the northernmost part of Scotland. Featuring bright neons on a black background using the stranding technique, this sweater will also help practise simple increases.

Measurements
See chart below

What you will need
- Rowan Big Wool
  100% merino wool
  80m (87 yards) per 100g (3½ oz)
Quantity:
- **A** 5[5:6:7:7] x 100g (3½ oz) balls in Black
- **B** 1[1:1:1:1] x 100g (3½ oz) ball in Oasis
- **C** 1[1:1:1:1] x 100g (3½ oz) ball in Cerise
- **D** 1[1:1:1:1] x 100g (3½ oz) ball in Midori
- **E** 1[1:1:1:1] x 100g (3½ oz) ball in Steel Blue
- **F** 1[1:1:1:1] x 100g (3½ oz) ball in Citron

- 10mm (US 15) circular needle, 40cm (16 in), 60cm (24 in), 80cm (32 in) and 100cm (40 in) length
- Stitch markers
- Stitch holders
- Yarn needle

Tension (gauge)
9 sts and 10 rounds to 10cm (4 in) meas over St st on 10mm (US 15) needles. Change needle size as necessary to achieve correct tension (gauge).

Abbreviations
See page 61.
MB: make bobble as (k1, p1) twice all into next st, turn and p4, turn and sl2k, k2tog, pass the 2 slipped sts over (bobble completed)

Special techniques
Working in the round (see pages 100–101).
Stranding (see page 131).
Picking up stitches (see page 155).

Adult size	XS	S/M	L/XL	XXL	XXXL	
To fit chest	71–86	91.5–106.5	111.5–117	122–137	142–158	cm
	28–34	36–42	44–46	48–54	56–62	in
Actual chest	124.5	133.5	142	151	160	cm
	49	52½	56	59½	63	in
Length	54	58	60	64	68	cm
	21¼	22¾	23½	25¼	26¾	in
Sleeve length	50	51	51	52	52	cm
	19¾	20	20	20½	20½	in

Notes

Joining a new colour in the round to avoid the jog
1. Patt first round in new colour. Insert working needle in RH leg of first stitch in row below and lift it onto LH needle.
2. Insert working needle in first stitch of last round and stitch below and knit the 2 stitches together.

Needle lengths

Change to longer circular needles as required when increasing stitches for the yoke. When you separate the sleeves from the body you may prefer to change back to a shorter needle for the body.

To make

Yoke

Note: Begins at neck edge at centre back. Using 10mm (US 15) 40cm (16 in) circular needle and **A**, cast on 40[42:44:46:48] sts. Place marker to show beg of round and join to work in the round, ensuring sts are not twisted.
Round 1: *K1, p1, rep from * to end of round.
Work 1 round more in rib as set.
Change to **B** and work 2 rounds in rib.
Change to **A** and work 2 rounds in rib.
Change to **C** and work 2 rounds in rib.
Change to **A** and work 2 rounds in rib.

Work yoke chart

Changing needle length as necessary and working from yoke chart Rounds 1 to 26, continue as follows to shape yoke, noting that pattern repeat is shown on chart with a red outline, and working increases for each size as given below:

Size XS only

Round 2: (K1, m1, k1) 20 times. *60 sts.*
Round 8: K6, (m1, k1) 48 times, k6. *108 sts.*
Round 12: K6, (m1, k5) 20 times, k2. *128 sts.*
Round 15: K7, (m1, k6) 20 times, k1. *148 sts.*
Round 18: K7, (m1, k5) 28 times, k1. *176 sts.*

Size S/M only
Round 2: (M1, k2) 10 times, m1, k1, (m1, k2) 10 times, m1, k1. *64 sts.*
Round 8: *(M1, k2) 4 times, (m1, k1) 15 times, (m1, k2) 4 times, m1, k1, rep from * once more. *112 sts.*
Round 12: *K2, (m1, k5, m1, k4) 6 times, m1, rep from * once more. *136 sts.*
Round 15: *K2, (m1, k6, m1, k5) 6 times, m1, rep from * once more. *160 sts.*
Round 18: *K2, (m1, k7, m1, k6) 6 times, m1, rep from * once more. *184 sts.*

Size L/XL only
Round 2: *(M1, k2) 5 times, m1, k1, (m1, k2) 5 times, m1, k1, rep from * once more. *68 sts.*
Round 8: *(M1, k2) 5 times, (m1, k1) 13 times, (m1, k2) 5 times, m1, k1, rep from * once more. *116 sts.*
Round 12: *K2, (m1, k5) 5 times, m1, k4, (m1, k5) 5 times, m1, k2, rep from * once more. *140 sts.*
Round 15: K2, (k1, m1, k4) 27 times, m1, k3. *168 sts.*
Round 18: K6, (k1, m1, k4) 32 times, k2. *200 sts.*

Size XXL only
Round 2: *(M1, k2) 5 times, (m1, k1) twice, (m1, k2) 5 times, m1, k1, rep from * once more. *72 sts.*
Round 8: *(M1, k2) 4 times, (m1, k1) 19 times, (m1, k2) 4 times, m1, k1, rep from * once more. *128 sts.*
Round 12: *K4, (m1, k5) 12 times, rep from * once more. *152 sts.*
Round 15: *K5, (m1, k5) 14 times, k1, rep from * once more. *180 sts.*
Round 18: *K6, (m1, k6) 14 times, rep from * once more. *208 sts.*

Size XXXL only
Round 2: *(M1, k2) 5 times, (m1, k1) 3 times, (m1, k2) 5 times, m1, k1, rep from * once more. *76 sts.*
Round 8: *(M1, k2) 5 times, (m1, k1) 17 times, (m1, k2) 5 times, m1, k1, rep from * once more. *132 sts.*
Round 12: *K5, (m1, k5) 12 times, k1, rep from * once more. *156 sts.*
Round 15: *K6, (m1, k5) 14 times, k2, rep from * once more. *184 sts.*
Round 18: *K2, (m1, k6) 6 times, (m1, k5) 3 times, (m1, k6) 6 times, m1, k3, rep from * once more. *216 sts.*

Sizes L/XL, XXL and XXXL only
Knit 1 round in **D**.

Sizes XXL and XXXL only
Knit 1 round in **A**.

All sizes
Divide for body and sleeves
Set up round: Working in **D[D:A:A:A]**, k26[28:30:32:34] for first half of back, leave next 36[36:40:40:40] sts on a holder for sleeve, using backwards loop method cast on 4 sts for underarm, patt 52[56:60:64:68] for front, leave next 36[36:40:40:40] sts on a holder for sleeve, using backwards loop method cast on 4 sts, patt 26[28:30:32:34]. *112[120:128:136:144] sts.*

Body

Using **A**, knit 20[24:25:28:32] rounds.
Work in k1, p1 rib as follows:
2 rounds **A**
2 rounds **F**
2 rounds **A**
2 rounds **D**
2 rounds **A**
Cast off (bind off) in rib.

Sleeves (both alike)

Using 10mm (US 15) needles 40cm (16in) length and with **A** and right side of work facing, starting halfway across underarm cast-on edge, pick up and knit 2 sts, k36[36:40:40:40] sts from sleeve holder, pick up and knit 2 sts from rem underarm cast-on edge. Place marker to show beg of round and join to work in the round. *40[40:44:44:44] sts.*
Using **A**, knit 33[34:34:35:35] rounds.

Work sleeve chart
Beginning each round with stitch 1[1:7:7:7] and ending with stitch 8[8:2:2:2], work from sleeve chart Rounds 1 to 5 as set.
Next round (dec): Using **A**, *K2, k2tog, rep from * to end of round. *30[30:33:33:33] sts.*
Work in k1, p1 rib as follows:
2 rounds **A**, while dec 0[0:1:1:1] st on 1st round. *30[30:32:32:32] sts.*
2 rounds **C**
2 rounds **A**
2 rounds **B**
2 rounds **A**
Cast off (bind off) in rib.

Sleeve chart

 With A, knit on RS rows

 With F, knit on RS rows

To finish

Weave in any yarn ends.
Gently steam on reverse.

Masterclass

Stranding

The bands of colour motifs around the yoke and cuffs of this sweater are knitted using the stranded colourwork technique. As the sweater is knitted in stocking (stockinette) stitch in the round, you knit every stitch while alternating colours, following the charts showing the placement of the colour stitches.

The bands of motifs in Fair Isle designs only ever use two colours, and so when working stranded colourwork you need to carry the strand of yarn not in use across the back of the fabric until you need to use it again. This results in strands of yarn laying across the wrong side of the work, which are known as floats, and is done to keep strand neat and prevent the fabric from puckering. The most important thing when stranding yarns across your work is to maintain an even tension with the floats. They must be long enough to span the width of the stitches they are sitting behind, even when the knitted fabric is slightly stretched, but not so loose that the stitches lose definition.

Knitters often knit stranded colourwork with a tighter tension (gauge) than usual, tightening up because of all the switches between different yarns. Going up a needle size for the stranded colourwork bands can be a good idea and helps to compensate for this natural tightening of tension. Another tip for achieving a good tension is to spread out the stitches just worked on the right needle each time you switch to a different colour yarn. If the knitted stitches are all bunched up together, the float at the back of the work will be too short. If they are spread out, the float will span the full width of those stitches and the fabric will be less likely to pucker.

Stranding on a knit row

One   On a knit row, drop the working yarn. Bring the new colour over the top of the dropped yarn and work to the next colour change.

Two   Drop the working yarn. Bring the new colour under the dropped yarn and work to the next colour change. Repeat these two steps for all subsequent colour changes.

Varsity Cardigan

Inspired by 1950s letterman jackets, this classic cardigan is sporty with a vintage twist. Knitted in three colours, with patch pockets and asymmetric stripe detailing in the rib buttonbands, hem and cuffs. Using embroidery and applique letters oversewn on to the front, make it unique to you. Knitted in a recycled cotton yarn, this jacket is perfect for warm spring days and chilly summer evenings, with the added cool factor of being planet friendly too.

Measurements
See chart below for adult sizes and see chart on page 138 for junior sizes

What you will need
- Kremke Soul Wool Karma Cotton 70% cotton, 30% recycled polyamide 105m (114 yards) per 50g (1¾ oz)

ADULT SIZE Quantity:
- **A** 3[3:4:4:4] x 50g (1¾ oz) balls in Black
- **B** 8[8:9:10:11] x 50g (1¾ oz) balls in Orange
- **C** 1[1:1:1:1] x 50g (1¾ oz) ball in Aquamarine

JUNIOR SIZE Quantity:
- **A** 2[2:3] x 50g (1¾ oz) balls in Violet
- **B** 3[4:5] x 50g (1¾ oz) balls in Lime
- **C** 1[1:1] x 50g (1¾ oz) ball in Deep Pink
- 1 pair 4mm (US 6) knitting needles
- 3.75mm (US 5) circular needle, 80cm (32 in) length
- Stitch holders
- Stitch markers
- 2 small buttons approx. 11mm (½ in) (for adult size only)
- 4 large buttons approx. 20mm (¾ in)
- Yarn needle

Tension (gauge)
18 sts and 26 rows to 10cm (4 in) over St st on 4mm (US 6) needles. Change needle size as necessary to achieve correct tension (gauge).

Abbreviations
See page 61.

Special techniques
Short-row shaping (see pages 90–91)
Adding surface embroidery (see page 141)

Adult sizes	XS	S/M	L/XL	XXL	XXXL	
To fit chest	71–86	91.5–106.5	111.5–117	122–137	142–158	cm
	28–34	36–42	44–46	48–54	56–62	in
Actual chest	104.5	115.5	129	144.5	160	cm
	41¼	45½	50¾	57	63	in
Length	61	63	65	67	69	cm
	24	24¾	25½	26¼	27	in
Sleeve length	45.5	47	47	48	48	cm
	18	18½	18½	19	19	in

To make adult size

Hem and cuff stripe sequence	Body stripe sequence
6 rows **A**	4 rows **A**
2 rows **B**	2 rows **B**
4 rows **A**	24 rows **A**
2 rows **B**	2 rows **B**
6 rows **A**	4 rows **A**

Back

Using 4mm (US 6) needles and **A**, cast on 96[106:118:132:146] sts and follow hem and cuff stripe sequence above work in rib as follows.
Rib row: *K1, p1, rep from * to end of row.
Work 19 more rows in rib as set.
Using **B** and beg with a knit row, work 54[56:58:62:64] rows in St st, ending with RS facing for next row. Work should meas 28[29:30:31:32] cm (11[11½:11¾:12¼:12½] in) from cast-on edge.
Continue in St st and follow body stripe sequence above, and placing markers at both sides when work meas 38[39:40:41:42] cm (15[15¼:15¾:16¼:16½] in) from cast-on edge to show start of armholes.
Using **B**, work 48[50:54:56:58] rows straight, ending with RS facing for next row. Work should meas 60[62:64:66:68] cm (23½[24½:25¼:26:26¾] in) from cast-on edge.

Shape shoulders
Next row (RS): Knit to last 8[10:11:13:15] sts, wrap next st and turn.
Next row: Purl to last 8[10:11:13:15] sts, wrap next st and turn.
Next row: Knit to last 17[20:22:26:29] sts, wrap next st and turn.
Next row: Purl to last 17[20:22:26:29] sts, wrap next st and turn.
Next row: Knit to last 25[29:33:38:43] sts, wrap next st and turn.
Next row: Purl to last 25[29:33:38:43] sts, wrap next st and turn.
Next row: K8[9:10:12:13], turn.
Next row: Purl across all 33[38:43:50:56] sts, picking up wraps as you work.
Cut yarn leaving a long end.
Slip these 33[38:43:50:56] sts onto a stitch holder for shoulder.
With RS of work facing, slip centre 30[30:32:32:34] sts onto a stitch holder.
Rejoin yarn to rem 33[38:43:50:56] sts. Knit across all sts, picking up wraps as you work.
Cut yarn leaving a long end.
Slip these 33[38:43:50:56] sts onto a stitch holder for shoulder.

Left front

Using 4mm (US 6) needles and **A**, cast on 45[50:56:63:70] sts and follow hem and cuff stripe sequence above work in rib as follows:
Sizes XS and XXL only
Rib row 1: K1, *p1, k1, rep from * to end of row.
Rib row 2: P1, *k1, p1, rep from * to end of row.
Sizes S/M, L/XL and XXXL only
Rib row 1: *P1, k1, rep from * to end of row.
Rib row 2: As Rib row 1.
All sizes
Continue in rib as set for 18 rows more.
Using **B** and beg with a knit row, work 54[56:58:62:64] rows in St st, ending with RS facing for next row.
Work should meas 28[29:30:31:32] cm (11[11½:11¾:12¼:12½] in) from cast-on edge.
Continue in St st and follow body stripe sequence above for 22[22:22:26:28] rows, ending with RS of work facing for next row.

Shape front neck
Left neck decreases are worked as follows:
RS row dec: Knit to last 5 sts, k2tog, k3.
WS row dec: P3, p2tog, purl to end of row.

Starting with a RS row dec, dec as above on next and every following 5th[5th:5th:5th:4th] row, while completing body stripe sequence. When stripes are complete, continue in **B** only, shaping neck edge as set until 33[38:43:50:56] sts rem, and placing a marker at side edge when work meas 38[39:40:41:42] cm (15[15¼:15¾:16¼:16½] in) from cast-on edge to show start of armhole. Work 7[9:8:6:14] rows straight, ending with WS facing for next row.

Shape shoulder

Next row (WS): Purl to last 8[10:11:13:15] sts, wrap next st and turn.
Next row: Knit to end of row.
Next row: Purl to last 17[20:22:26:29] sts, wrap next st and turn.
Next row: Knit to end of row.
Next row: Purl to last 25[29:33:38:43] sts, wrap next st and turn.
Next row: Knit to end of row.
Next row: Purl across all sts, picking up wraps as you work.
Cut yarn leaving a long end.
Slip these 33[38:43:50:56] sts onto a holder for shoulder.

Right front

Using 4mm (US 6) needles and **A**, cast on 45[50:56:63:70] sts and follow hem and cuff stripe sequence above work in rib as follows:
Sizes XS and XXL only
Rib row 1: K1, *p1, k1, rep from * to end of row.
Rib row 2: P1, *k1, p1, rep from * to end of row.
Sizes S/M, L/XL and XXXL only
Rib row 1: *K1, p1, rep from * to end of row.
Rib row 2: As Rib row 1.
All sizes
Continue in rib as set for 18 rows more.
Using **B** throughout and beg with a knit row work 76[78:80:88:92] rows in St st, ending with RS facing for next row.

Shape front neck

Right neck decreases are worked as follows:
RS row dec: K3, k2tog tbl, knit to end of row.
WS row dec: Purl to last 5 sts, p2tog tbl, p3.

Starting with a RS row dec, dec as above on next and every following 5th[5th:5th:5th:4th] row until 33[38:43:50:56] sts rem, and placing marker at side edge when work meas 38[39:40:41:42] cm (15[15¼:15¾:16¼:16½] in) from cast-on edge to show start of armhole.
Work 6[8:7:5:13] rows straight, ending with RS facing for next row.

Shape shoulder

Next row (RS): Knit to last 8[10:11:13:15] sts, wrap next st and turn.
Next row: Purl to end of row.
Next row: Knit to last 17[20:22:26:29] sts, wrap next st and turn.
Next row: Purl to end of row.
Next row: K to last 25[29:33:38:43] sts, wrap next st and turn.
Next row: Purl to end of row.
Next row: Knit across all sts, picking up wraps as you work.
Cut yarn leaving a long end.
Slip these 33[38:43:50:56] sts onto a holder for shoulder.
Using **B**, join both shoulders using three-needle cast off (bind off) method, with wrong sides of work together so seam is on outside of work.

Sleeves

Right sleeve stripe sequence
33[37:37:39:39] rows **B**
24 rows **C**
42 rows **B**

Left sleeve stripe sequence
53[57:57:59:59] rows **B**
6 rows **C**
6 rows **B**
6 rows **C**
28 rows **B**

Sleeve pattern
With RS facing, 4mm (US 6) needles and **B**, pick up and knit 80[84:88:90:94] sts evenly between armhole markers.
Beg with a purl row and working in correct sleeve stripe sequence above, work 5 rows in St st, ending with RS facing for next row.
Next row (RS, dec): K3, k2tog, knit to last 5 sts, k2tog tbl, k3. *2 st dec.*
Work 4[4:3:3:3] rows straight.
Sizes XS and S only
Next row (WS, dec): P3, p2tog tbl, purl to last 5 sts, p2tog, p3. *2 st dec.*
Sizes M, L/XL and XXL only
Next row (RS, dec): K3, k2tog, knit to last 5 sts, k2tog tbl, k3. *2 st dec.*

All sizes

Dec as above on every following 5th[5th:4th:4th:4th] row until 42[46:46:48:50] sts rem. Continue straight in St st until sleeve stripe sequence completed.
Now follow hem and cuff stripe sequence, work in 1x1 rib as for back for 20 rows.
Cast off (bind off) in rib.

Pockets (make two)

Using 4mm (US 6) needles and **B**, cast on 25 sts and beg with a knit row, work 26 rows in St st, ending with RS facing for next row.
Next row (RS): *K1, p1, rep from * to last st, k1.
Next row: *P1, k1, rep from * to last st, p1.
Rep last 2 rows 4 times more.
Cast off (bind off) in rib.

Button band

Place markers counting from cast-on along left front for buttonhole placement and along right front for buttons as follows:

1st small buttonhole on row 6[6:6:6:6] from cast-on.
2nd small buttonhole on row 16[16:16:16:18].
3rd large buttonhole on row 27[29:31:31:35].
4th large buttonhole on row 49[51:53:55:59].
5th large buttonhole on row 71[73:75:79:83].
6th large buttonhole on row 93[95:97:103:107].

When indicated, work buttonholes as follows:
Small buttonholes
Row 1: Work to buttonhole marker, knit 2 together, yarn over.
Row 2: Work yarn over as a stitch on this row.

Large buttonholes
Row 1: Work to buttonhole marker, knit 2 together, yarn over twice, knit 2 together tbl.
Row 2: Work yarnovers as follows: purl into first yarn over and then purl into back of second yarn over.
Work in intarsia. When changing colour, always twist colours on WS of work.

With RS facing, 3.75mm (US 5) circular needle, and **B**, pick up and knit 123[127:129:133:137] sts up right front, 3 sts across right back neck, k30[30:32:32:34] sts from back holder, pick up and knit 4 sts across left back neck and 123[127:129:133:137] sts down left front. Do not join, work in rows. *283[291:297:305:315] sts.*

Row 1 (WS): Using **B**, *k1, p1, rep from * to left shoulder seam, place marker, change to **A** and continue in rib as set to last st, k1.
Row 2: Using **A** rib as set to marker, change to **B** and rib to end of row.
Row 3: Using **B** rib to marker, change to **A** and rib to end of row.
Row 4: Using **B** rib to marker, change to **C** and rib to end of row.
Row 5: Using **C** rib to first buttonhole marker, work row 1 of small buttonhole, rib to second marker and work row 1 of small buttonhole, rib to next buttonhole marker and work row 1 of large buttonhole, rep for rem 3 large buttonholes, rib to marker at shoulder, change to **A** and rib to end of row.
Row 6: Using **B** rib to marker, change to **C**

and work row 2 of buttonholes, rib to end of row.
Row 7: Using C rib to marker, change to **B** and rib to end of row.
Row 8: Using **B** rib as set to end of row, removing marker as you work.
Row 9: Using **B** rib as set to end of row. Cast off (bind off) in rib.

To make junior size

Junior size	2–3	4–5	6–7	years
Actual chest	70	76.5	81.5	cm
	27½	30	32	in
Length	36	38	40	cm
	14¼	15	15¾	in
Sleeve length	26	27	28	cm
	10¼	10¾	11	in

Hem and cuff stripe sequence	Body stripe sequence
4 rows **A**	2 rows **A**
2 rows **B**	2 rows **B**
2 rows **A**	16 rows **A**
2 rows **B**	2 rows **B**
4 rows **A**	2 rows **A**

Back

Using 4mm (US 6) needles and **A**, cast on 60[66:70] sts and foll hem and cuff stripe sequence above work in rib as follows:
Rib row: *K1, p1, rep from * to end of row.
Work 13 more rows in rib as set.
Using **B** and beg with a knit row, work 28[30:32] rows in St st, ending with RS facing for next row. Work should meas 16[17:17.5] cm (6¼[6¾:7] in) from cast-on edge.
Continue in St st and following body stripe sequence above, and placing markers at both sides when work meas 22[23:24] cm (8¾[9:9½] in) from cast-on edge to show start of armholes.
Using **B**, work 26[28:30] rows straight, ending with RS facing for next row. Work should meas 35[37:38.5] cm (13¾[14½:15¼] in) from cast-on edge.

Shape shoulders
Next row (RS): Knit to last 7[8:8] sts, wrap next st and turn.
Next row: Purl to last 7[8:8] sts, wrap next st and turn.
Next row: Knit to last 14[15:16] sts, wrap next st and turn.
Next row: Purl to last 14[15:16] sts, wrap next st and turn.
Next row: K6[7:7], turn.
Next row: Purl across all 20[22:23] sts, picking up wraps as you work.
Cut yarn leaving long end.
Slip the 20[22:23] sts onto a holder for shoulder.

With RS of work facing slip centre 20[22:24] sts onto a holder. Rejoin yarn to rem 20[22:23] sts and knit across all sts, picking up wraps as you work.
Cut yarn leaving long end.
Slip the 20[22:23] sts onto a holder for shoulder.

Left front

Using 4mm (US 6) needles and **A**, cast on 33[36:38] sts and follow hem and cuff stripe sequence above work in rib as follows:
Size 2–3 only
Rib row 1: K1, *p1, k1, rep from * to end of row.
Rib row 2: P1, *k1, p1, rep from * to end of row.
Sizes 4–5 and 6–7 only
Rib row 1: *P1, k1, rep from * to end of row.
Rib row 2: As Rib row 1.
All sizes
Continue in rib as set for 13 rows more.

Using **B** and beg with a knit row, work 28[30:32] rows in St st, ending with RS facing for next row. Work should meas 16[17:17.5] cm (6¼[6¾:7] in) from cast-on edge.
Cont in St st and follow body stripe sequence above for 14 rows, ending with RS of work facing for next row.

Shape front neck
Left neck decreases are worked as follows:
RS row dec: Knit to last 5 sts, k2tog, k3.
WS row dec: P3, p2tog, purl to end of row.
Starting with a RS row dec, dec as above

on next and 3[4:5] following alt rows, then on every foll 3rd row, while completing body stripe sequence. When stripes are complete, continue in **B** only, shaping neck edge as set until 20[22:23] sts rem, and placing marker at side edge when work meas 22[23:24] cm (8¾[9:9½] in) from cast-on edge to show start of armhole.
Work 1 row straight, ending with WS facing for next row.

Shape shoulder
Next row (WS): Purl to last 7[8:8] sts, wrap next st and turn.
Next row: Knit to end of row.
Next row: Purl to last 14[15:16] sts, wrap next st and turn.
Next row: Knit to end of row.
Next row: Purl across all sts, picking up wraps as you work.
Cut yarn leaving a long end.
Slip the 20[22:23] sts onto a holder for shoulder.

Right front

Using 4mm (US 6) needles and **A**, cast on 33[36:38] sts and follow hem and cuff stripe sequence above work in rib as follows:
Size 2–3 only
Rib row 1: K1, *p1, k1, rep from * to end of row.
Rib row 2: P1, *k1, p1, rep from * to end of row.
Sizes 4–5 and 6–7 only
Rib row 1: *K1, p1, rep from * to end of row.
Rib row 2: As Rib row 1.
All sizes
Continue in rib as set for 12 rows more.

Using B throughout and beg with a knit row, work 42[44:46] rows in St st, ending with RS facing for next row.

Shape front neck
Right neck decreases are worked as follows:
RS row dec: K3, k2tog tbl, knit to end of row.
WS row dec: Purl to last 5 sts, p2tog tbl, p3.
Starting with a RS row dec, dec as above on next and 3[4:5] foll alt rows, then on every foll 3rd row until 20[22:23] sts rem, and placing a marker at side edge when work

meas 22[23:24] cm (8¾[9:9½] in) from cast-on edge to show start of armhole.
Work 2 rows straight, ending with RS facing for next row.

Shape shoulder
Next row (RS): Knit to last 7[8:8] sts, wrap next st and turn.
Next row: Purl to end of row.
Next row: Knit to last 14[15:16] sts, wrap next st and turn.
Next row: Purl to end of row.
Next row: Knit across all sts, picking up wraps as you work.
Cut yarn leaving long end.
Slip the 20[22:23] sts onto a holder for shoulder.

Using B, join both shoulders using three-needle cast off (bind off) method, with wrong sides of work together so seam is on outside of your work.

Sleeves

Right sleeve stripe sequence
13[17:19] rows **B**
12 rows **C**
28 rows **B**

Left sleeve stripe sequence
33[37:39] rows **B**
4 rows **C**
2 rows **B**
4 rows **C**
10 rows **B**

Sleeve pattern
With RS facing, 4mm (US 6) needles and **B**, pick up and knit 50[54:56] sts evenly between armhole markers.
Beg with a purl row and working in correct sleeve stripe sequence above, work 13[3:7] rows in St st, ending with RS facing for next row.
Next row (RS, dec): K3, k2tog, knit to last 5 sts, k2tog tbl, k3.
Dec as above on every foll 4th[6th:6th] row until 34[38:40] sts rem.
Continue straight in St st until sleeve stripe sequence completed.
Now follow hem and cuff stripe sequence, work in 1x1 rib as for back for 14 rows.
Cast off (bind off) in rib.

Pockets (make two)

Using 4mm (US 6) needles and B, cast on 15 sts and beg with a knit row, work 16 rows in St st, ending with RS facing for next row.
Next row (RS): *K1, p1, rep from * to last st, k1.
Next row: *P1, k1, rep from * to last st, p1.
Repeat last 2 rows twice more.
Cast off (bind off) in rib.

Button band

Place markers counting from cast-on along left front for buttonhole placement and along right front for buttons as follows:
1st buttonhole on row 6[6:8] from cast-on.
2nd buttonhole on row 21[23:25].
3rd buttonhole on row 36[40:42].
4th buttonhole on row 51[57:59].

When indicated, work buttonholes as foll:
Row 1: Work to buttonhole marker, knit 2 together, yarn over.
Row 2: Work yarn over as a stitch on this row.

Work button band in intarsia. When changing colour, always twist colours on WS of work.

With RS facing, 3.75mm (US 5) circular needle and B, pick up and knit 73[77:81] sts up right front, 3 sts across right back neck, k20[22:24] sts from back holder, pick up and knit 4 sts across left back neck and 73[77:81] sts down left front. Do not join, work in rows. *173(183:193) sts.*
Row 1 (WS): Using B, *K1, p1, rep from * to left shoulder seam, place marker, change to A and continue in rib as set to last st, k1.
Row 2: Using A, rib as set to marker, change to B and rib to end of row.
Row 3: Using C, rib to first buttonhole marker, work row 1 of buttonhole, rib to second marker and work row 1 of buttonhole, rep for rem 2 buttonholes, rib to marker at shoulder, change to A and rib to end of row.
Row 4: Using B, rib to marker, change to C and work row 2 of buttonholes, rib to end of row.
Row 5: Using B, rib as set to end of row, removing marker as you work.
Row 6: Using B, rib as set to end of row.
Cast off (bind off) in rib.

To finish

Weave in any ends. Gently steam on reverse. Using leftover yarn C and photograph as a guide, use chain stitch to embroider "love" (or word of your choice) across band of colour A on back of cardigan. Use chain stitch and yarn C to embroider a heart just below centre top back neck. Weave in any ends on WS of work.
Customise cardigan with any appliqué letter of your choice, sewn to front of cardigan, approx. 16cm (6¼ in) down from top of shoulder for adult size and 11cm (4½in) down from top of shoulder for junior size, using oversew stitch and yarn A to contrast. Join side and sleeve seams.
For adult size, place each pocket approx. 9cm (3½ in) in from edge of button band and 8cm (3¼ in) up from cast-on edge, above rib.
For junior size, place each pocket approx. 6cm (2¼in) in from edge of button band and 5.5cm (2in) up from cast-on edge, above rib.
Pin and sew into position using mattress stitch or whip stitch.
Sew on buttons to match buttonholes.

Masterclass

Adding surface embroidery

Chain stitch is a versatile embroidery stitch, which is used to create curved, flowing lines. This makes it the perfect choice for the joined-up letters used on this cardigan.

One   Draw a motif or write a word onto your knitted fabric using a washable or fading fabric pen. Thread a blunt-tipped needle with a 40 cm (18 in) length of yarn and bring it up at the start point, leaving a tail at the back for weaving in later. Loop the yarn from left to right, then re-insert the needle at the start point and bring it out two stitches below.

Two   Pull the needle through the knitted fabric and out over the loop. Draw the yarn up gently to make a loop or "chain".

Three   Insert the needle inside the loop, ready to make the next stitch and bring the tip of the needle out the same distance below. Repeat the first two steps and continue to the end of the line drawn line, keeping the stitches even and regular. Finish off by anchoring the final loop down with a small straight stitch. Weave the ends in at the back, along the back of the embroidery.

Swirl Vest

With fluid swirls of colour that remind me of a summer sunset, this sleeveless vest is a versatile piece to be worn on its own or layered up. In this pattern you will work from a chart using the intarsia technique, which begins in the rib hem. Sleeveless with a raw edge armhole, this fuzzy mohair vest is perfect if you don't enjoy knitting sleeves!

Measurements
See chart below

Materials
- Debbie Bliss Nell
  78% mohair, 13% merino wool,
  9% polyamide
  100m (109 yards) per 50g (1¾ oz)

Quantity:
- **A** 2[3:3:3:4] x 50g (1¾ oz) balls in Heather
- **B** 3[3:4:4:5] x 50g (1¾ oz) balls in Lilac
- **C** 2[2:2:3:3] x 50g (1¾ oz) balls in Corn
- **D** 1[1:1:2:2] x 50g (1¾ oz) ball(s) in Sunset
- **E** 1[1:1:1:1] x 50g (1¾ oz) ball in Jade
- **F** 1[1:1:1:1] x 50g (1¾ oz) ball in Rose
- **G** 1[1:1:2:2] x 50g (1¾ oz) ball(s) in Willow

- 1 pair of 6mm (US 10) knitting needles
- 6mm (US 10) circular needle, 40cm (16 in) length
- Stitch markers
- Stitch holders
- Yarn needle

Tension (gauge)
13 sts and 17 rows to 10cm (4 in) over St st using 6mm (US 10) needles. Change needle size as necessary to achieve correct tension (gauge).

Abbreviations
See page 61.

Special techniques
Working intarsia (see page 149).
Short-row shaping (see pages 90–91).

Note
Back and front are worked using the intarsia colourwork method.

Adult size	XS	S	M	L/XL	XXL	
To fit chest	71–86	91.5–106.5	111.5–117	122–137	142–158	cm
	28–34	36–42	44–46	48–54	56–62	in
Actual chest	89	104.5	123	138.5	154	cm
	35	41¼	48½	54½	60¾	in
Length	52	54	56.5	57.5	60	cm
	20½	21¼	22¼	22¾	23½	in

To make

Back

Using 6mm (US 10) needles and **A**, cast on 56[66:78:86:96] sts.
Now work from Back chart, changing colour and working in intarsia where indicated and working first 11[11:13:13:15] rows of chart in k1, p1 rib.
When working from chart and working in k1, p1 rib, beg RS rows on stitch 24[19:13:9:4] and knit until you have completed stitch 79[84:90:94:99]. Beg WS rows on stitch 79[84:90:94:99] and purl until you have completed stitch 24[19:13:9:4].
When Row 11[11:13:13:15] of chart is complete, increase as follows:
Next row (WS inc): (Rib 11[13:16:12:14], m1) 4[4:4:6:6] times, rib to end of row.
60[70:82:92:102] sts.
After you have completed this increase row, when working from chart beg RS rows on stitch 22[17:11:6:1] and knit until you have completed stitch 81[86:92:97:102]. Beg WS rows on stitch 81[86:92:97:102] and purl until you have completed stitch 22[17:11:6:1].
Now beg with a knit row, continue in St st, placing markers at both sides on Row 53[55:57:57:59] to show start of armholes, until Row 88[92:96:98:102] has been completed, ending with RS facing for next row.

Shape shoulders and back neck
Next row (RS): Knit to last 5[7:8:9:10] sts, wrap next st and turn.
Next row: Purl to last 5[7:8:9:10] sts, wrap next st and turn.
Next row: Knit to last 11[14:18:20:21] sts, wrap next st and turn.
Next row: Purl to last 11[14:18:20:21] sts, wrap next st and turn.
Next row: K1[3:3:6:9], k2tog, k3, turn.
Next row: Purl across all 16[21:25:30:34] sts, picking up wraps as you work.
Cut yarn leaving a long end.
Slip these 16[21:25:30:34] sts onto a stitch holder for shoulder.

With RS facing, slip centre 26[26:30:30:32] sts onto a holder. Rejoin yarn to rem sts and work as follows:
Next row: K3, k2tog tbl, knit to end of row picking up wraps as you work.
Cut yarn leaving a long end.
Slip these 16[21:25:30:34] sts onto a stitch holder for shoulder.

Front

Using 6mm (US 10) needles and **A**, cast on 56[66:78:86:96] sts.
Now work from Front chart, changing colour and working in intarsia where indicated and working the first 11[11:13:13:15] rows of chart in k1, p1 rib.
When working from chart and working in k1, p1 rib, begin RS rows on stitch 24[19:13:9:4] and knit until you have completed stitch 79[84:90:94:99]. Begin WS rows on stitch 79[84:90:94:99] and purl until you have completed stitch 24[19:13:9:4].
When Row 11[11:13:13:15] of chart is complete, increase as follows:
Next row (WS inc): (Rib 11[13:16:12:14], m1) 4[4:4:6:6] times, rib to end of row.
60[70:82:92:102] sts.
After you have completed this increase row, when working from Front chart begin RS rows on stitch 22[17:11:6:1] and knit until you have completed stitch 81[86:92:97:102]. Begin WS rows on stitch 81[86:92:97:102] and purl until you have completed stitch 22[17:11:6:1].
Now, beg with a knit row, continue in St st, placing markers at both sides on Row 53[55:57:57:59] to show start of armholes, until Row 84[88:92:94:98] has been completed, ending with RS facing for next row.

Shape neck and shoulders
Next row (RS): K16[21:25:30:34] sts, k2tog, k3, turn leaving rem sts on a holder.
Next row: P3, p2tog, purl to end of row.
Next row: Knit to last 5 sts, k2tog, k3.

Next row: Purl to end of row.
Next row: Knit to last 5 sts, k2tog, K3.
Next row: Purl to last 5[7:8:9:10] sts, wrap next st and turn.
Next row: Knit to last 5 sts, k2tog, k3.
Next row: Purl to last 11[14:18:20:21] sts, wrap next st and turn.
Next row: Knit to end of row.
Next row: Purl to end of row picking up wraps as you work.
Cut yarn leaving a long end.
Slip these 16[21:25:30:34] sts onto a holder for shoulder.
With RS facing, slip centre 18[18:22:22:24] sts onto a holder. Rejoin yarn to rem sts and work as follows:
Next row (RS): K3, k2tog tbl, knit to end of row.
Next row: Purl to last 5 sts, p2tog tbl, p3.
Next row: K3, k2tog tbl, knit to end of row.
Next row: Purl to end of row.
Next row: K3, k2tog tbl, knit to last 5[7:8:9:10] sts, wrap next st and turn.
Next row: Purl to end of row.
Next row: K3, k2tog tbl, knit to last 11[14:18:20:21] sts, wrap next st and turn.
Next row: Purl to end of row.
Next row: Knit to end of row picking up wraps as you work.
Cut yarn leaving a long end.
Slip these 16[21:25:30:34] sts onto a holder for shoulder.
Join both shoulders using three-needle cast-off (bind-off) method with wrong sides of work tog so seam is on outside of work.

Neckband

With RS facing, 6mm (US 10) circular needle and **C**, and starting at left shoulder, pick up and knit 10 sts down left front neck, k18[18:22:22:24] sts from front holder, pick up and knit 10 sts up right front neck, 3 sts across right back neck, k26[26:30:30:32] sts from back holder, pick up and knit 3 sts across left back neck, pm to show start of round. *70[70:78:78:82] sts.*
Work in the round as follows:
Next round: *K1, p1, rep from * to end of round.
Repeat last round 4 times more.
Next round (inc): Inc 1 st at both ends of round. *72[72:80:80:84] sts.*
Continue in rows in rib as set and intarsia method using **F** and **C** as follows:
Next row (RS): Rib 3[3:4:4:4] in **F**, rib in **C** to last 6[6:7:7:7] sts, rib 6[6:7:7:7] in **F**.
Next row: Rib 7[7:8:8:8] in **F**, rib in **C** to last 7[7:8:8:8] sts, rib 7[7:8:8:8] **F**.
Next row: Rib 13[13:14:14:15] in **F**, rib in **C** to last 7[7:8:8:9] sts, rib 7[7:8:8:9] in **F**.
Next row: Rib 10[10:12:12:13] in **F**, rib in **C** to last 16[16:17:17:18] sts, rib 16[16:17:17:18] in **F**.
Next row: Rib 19[19:21:21:22] in **F**, rib in **C** to last 15[15:17:17:18] sts, rib 15[15:17:17:18] in **F**.
Next row: Rib 19[19:21:21:22] in **F**, rib in **C** to last 21[21:22:22:23] sts, rib 21[21:22:22:23] in **F**.
Cast off (bind off) in rib in colours as set by last row.

To finish

Weave in any yarn ends.
Join side seams by matching markers.
Using **C** join the row ends on the neckband.

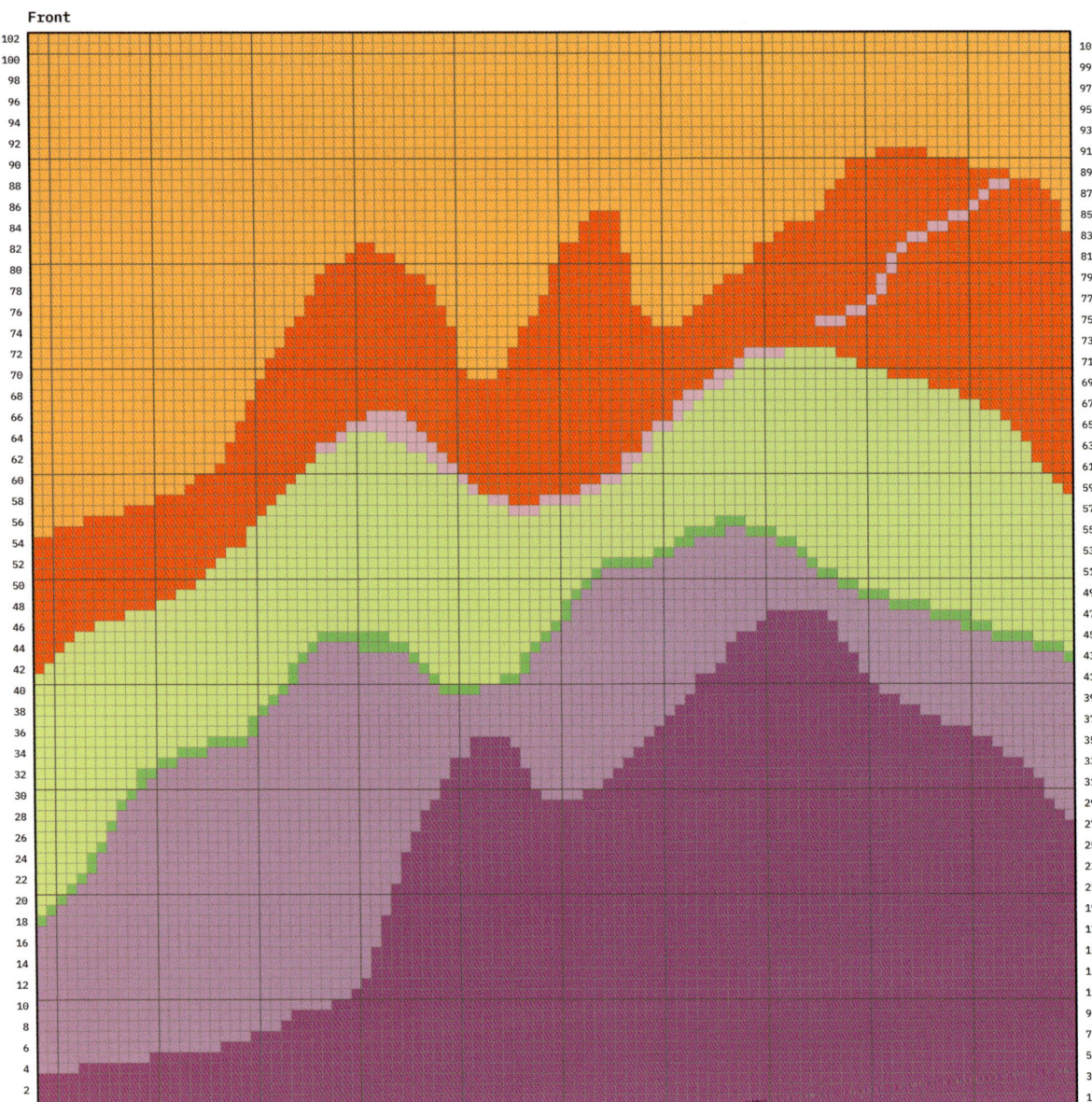

Front

- With A, knit on RS rows and purl on WS rows.
- With B, knit on RS rows and purl on WS rows.
- With C, knit on RS rows and purl on WS rows.
- With D, knit on RS rows and purl on WS rows.
- With E, knit on RS rows and purl on WS rows.
- With F, knit on RS rows and purl on WS rows.
- With G, knit on RS rows and purl on WS rows.

Knitted Garments

Back

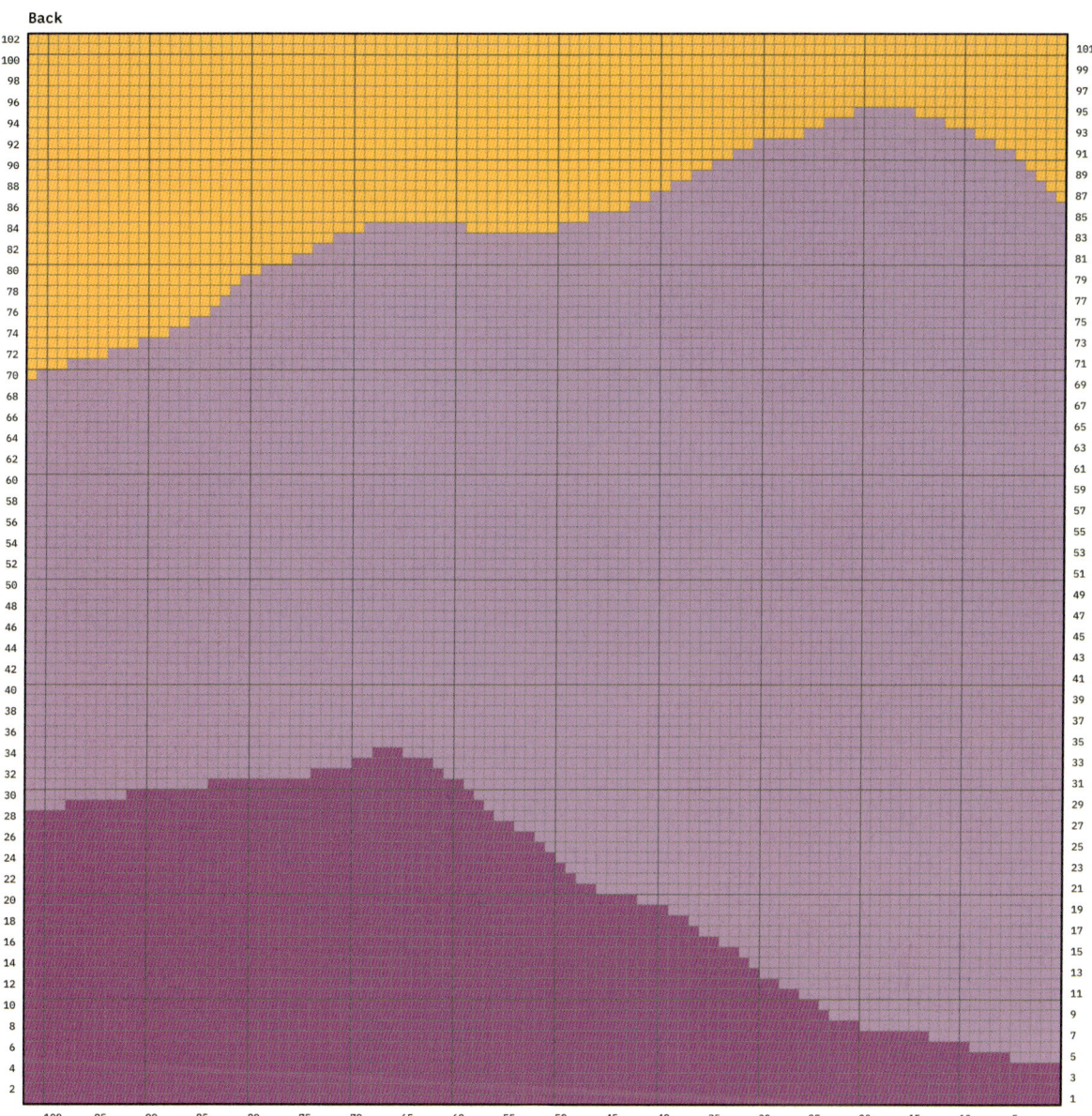

■ With A, knit on RS rows and purl on WS rows.
■ With B, knit on RS rows and purl on WS rows.
■ With G, knit on RS rows and purl on WS rows.

Knitted Garments

Masterclass

Working intarsia

When switching from using one colour yarn to a second colour yarn within the same row, you need to "twist" those yarns together to avoid making a hole in the knitted fabric. In effect, you are "twisting" the two colour yarns to link them together. Be careful not to overtwist the yarn or the fabric will not lie flat. The object is to link together the two separate colour sections so that they form a single fabric.

One   To join in a new colour on a knit row, work up to the colour change. Drop the old colour. Pick up the new colour from under the old colour and knit to the next colour change.

Two   On a purl row, work up to the colour change. Drop the old colour. Pick up the new colour from under the old colour and purl to the next colour change.

When knitting using several colours across a row, organise the yarns into "bobbins" – small windings of individual yarns. To work out how much yarn you will need, calculate the number of stitches that specific area then twist the yarn around the knitting needle that number of times, adding a small amount more for sewing in ends. Once you have measured out the correct amount of yarn, either wind it into a small bobbin by hand or wrap it around a shop-bought bobbin.

EASY

Balloon Sleeve Cardigan

A simple edge-to-edge cardigan with dramatic balloon-shaped cuffs, this easy to knit project creates a big impact. Designed to be cropped to sit at the waist, for a flattering fit. I love the back neck detail where the two fronts meet at the centre of the back neck for a neat and comfortable finish when worn.

Measurements
See chart below

What you will need
- Debbie Bliss Nell
  78% mohair, 13% merino wool, 9% polyamide
  100m (109 yards) per 50g (1¾ oz)

Quantity:
- 7[7:8:9:9] x 50g (1¾ oz) balls in Lilac
- 1 pair 6mm (US 10) knitting needles
- Stitch markers
- Stitch holders
- Yarn needle

Tension (gauge)
13 sts and 17 rows to 10cm (4 in) over St st stitch using 6mm (US 10) needles. Change needle size as necessary to achieve correct tension (gauge).

Abbreviations
See page 61.

Special technique
Short-row shaping (see pages 90–91).

Adult size	XS	S/M	L/XL	XXL	XXXL	
To fit chest	71–86	91.5–106.5	111.5–117	122–137	142–156	cm
	28–34	36–42	44–46	48–54	56–61	in
Actual chest	117	126	138.5	147.5	157	cm
	46	49½	54½	58	61¾	in
Length	50	52	54	56	58	cm
	19¾	20½	21¼	22	22¾	in
Sleeve length	45	45	45	43	43	cm
	17¾	17¾	17¾	17	17	in

Knitted Garments

To make

Back

Using 6mm (US 10) needles, cast on 78[84:92:98:104] sts.
Next row: *K1, p1, rep from * to end of row.
Repeat last row 11 times more.
Beg with a knit row, cont in St st until work meas 41[43:45:47:49]cm (16¼[17:17¾:18½:19¼] in) from cast-on edge, ending with RS facing for next row and placing markers at both sides when work meas 16[17:18:19:20]cm (6¼[6¾:7:7½:7¾] in) from cast-on edge, to mark start of armholes.

Shape shoulders

Next row (RS): Knit to last 5[6:7:8:9] sts, wrap next st and turn.
Next row: Purl to last 5[6:7:8:9] sts, wrap next st and turn.
Next row: Knit to last 9[12:13:14:16] sts, wrap next st and turn.
Next row: Purl to last 9[12:13:14:16] sts, wrap next st and turn.
Next row: Knit to last 14[17:19:20:22] sts, wrap next st and turn.
Next row: Purl to last 14[17:19:20:22] sts, wrap next st and turn.
Next row: Knit to last 19[22:25:26:28] sts, wrap next st and turn.
Next row: Purl to last 19[22:25:26:28] sts, wrap next st and turn.
Next row: Knit to last 24[27:31:32:34] sts, wrap next st and turn.
Next row: Purl to last 24[27:31:32:34] sts, wrap next st and turn.
Next row: Knit to last 29[32:36:38:40] sts, wrap next st and turn.
Next row: Purl to last 29[32:36:38:40] sts, wrap next st and turn.
Next row: Knit to last 34[37:41:44:46] sts, wrap next st and turn.
Next row: Purl to last 34[37:41:44:46] sts, wrap next st and turn.
Next row: K5[5:5:5:6], turn and purl across all sts picking up wraps as you work.
Cut yarn leaving a long end.
Slip these 39[42:46:49:52] sts onto a holder for shoulder.
With RS facing, rejoin yarn to rem sts and knit across all sts picking up wraps as you work.
Cut yarn leaving a long end.
Slip these 39[42:46:49:52] sts onto a holder for shoulder.

Right front

Using 6mm (US 10) needles, cast on 39[42:46:49:52] sts and work as follows:
Next row: *P1, k1, rep from * to last 1[0:0:1:0] st, p1[0:0:1:0].
Next row: K1[0:0:1:0], *p1, k1, rep from * to end of row.
Work a further 10 rows in rib as set.
Cont in St st with rib edges as follows:
Next row (RS): (P1, k1) 5 times, p1, knit to end of row.
Next row: Purl to last 11 sts, (k1, p1) 5 times, k1.
Repeat last 2 rows until work meas 41[43:45:47:49]cm (16¼[17:17¾:18½:19¼] in) from cast-on edge, ending with RS facing for next row and placing marker at side edge when work meas 16[17:18:19:20]cm (6¼[6¾:7:7½:7¾] in) from cast-on edge.

Shape shoulder

Next row: Patt to last 5[6:7:8:9] sts, wrap next st and turn.
Next row: Patt as set.
Next row: Patt to last 9[12:13:14:16] sts, wrap next st and turn.
Next row: Patt as set.
Next row: Patt to last 14[17:19:20:22] sts, wrap next st and turn.
Next row: Patt as set.
Next row: Patt to last 19[22:25:26:28] sts, wrap next st and turn.
Next row: Patt as set.
Next row: Patt to last 24[27:31:32:34] sts, wrap next st and turn.
Next row: Patt as set.
Next row: Patt to last 29[32:36:38:40] sts, wrap next st and turn.

Next row: Patt as set.
Next row: Patt to last 34[37:41:44:46] sts, wrap next st and turn.
Next row: Patt 5[5:5:5:6], turn and patt across all sts picking wraps up as you work. Cut yarn leaving a long end.
Slip these 39[42:46:49:52] sts onto a holder for shoulder.

Left front

Using 6mm (US 10) needles, cast on 39[42:46:49:52] sts and work as follows:
Next row: P1[0:0:1:0], *k1, p1, rep from * to end of row.
Next row: *K1, p1, rep from * to last 1[0:0:1:0] st, k1[0:0:1:0].
Work a further 10 rows in rib as set.
Cont in St st with rib edge as follows:
Next row (RS): Knit to last 11 sts, (p1, k1) 5 times, p1.
Next row: (K1, p1) 5 times, k1, purl to end of row.
Repeat last 2 rows until work meas 41[43:45:47:49]cm (16¼[17:17¾:18½:19¼] in) from cast-on edge, ending with WS facing for next row and placing marker at side edge when work meas 16[17:18:19:20]cm (6¼[6¾:7:7½:7¾] in) from cast-on edge.

Shape shoulder
Next row (WS): Patt to last 5[6:7:8:9] sts, wrap next st and turn.
Next row: Patt as set.
Next row: Patt to last 9[12:13:14:16] sts, wrap next st and turn.
Next row: Patt as set.
Next row: Patt to last 14[17:19:20:22] sts, wrap next st and turn.
Next row: Patt as set.
Next row: Patt to last 19[22:25:26:28] sts, wrap next st and turn.
Next row: Patt as set.
Next row: Patt to last 24[27:31:32:34] sts, wrap next st and turn.
Next row: Patt as set.
Next row: Patt to last 29[32:36:38:40] sts, wrap next st and turn.
Next row: Patt as set.
Next row: Patt to last 34[37:41:44:46] sts, wrap next st and turn.
Next row: Patt 5[5:5:5:6], turn and patt across all sts picking wraps up as you work. Cut yarn leaving a long end.
Slip these 39[42:46:49:52] sts onto a holder for shoulder.
Join shoulders using three-needle cast off (bind off) method with wrong sides of work tog so seams are on outside of your work.

Sleeves (both alike)

With RS facing and 6mm (US 10) needles, pick up and knit 62[64:68:70:72] sts evenly between markers.
Starting with a purl row, work 3 rows in St st, ending with RS facing for next row.
Next row (RS inc): K3, m1, knit to last 3 sts, m1, k3. *2 sts inc.*
Inc as above on every foll 4th[4th:6th:4th:6th] row until 80[84:84:88:88] sts.
Cont straight until sleeve meas 35[35:35:33:33]cm (13¾[13¾:13¾:13:13] in) from pick-up, ending with RS facing for next row.
Next row (RS dec): K1, *k2tog, rep from * to last st, k1. *41[43:43:45:45] sts.*
Next row: Purl.
Next row: *K1, p1, rep from * to last st, k1.
Next row: *P1, k1, rep from * to last st, p1.
Rep last 2 rows 6 times more.
Cast off (bind off) in rib.

To finish

Weave in any yarn ends.
Join side and sleeve seams.

Masterclass

Picking up stitches

When adding to a piece of knitting, like working the sleeves of this cardigan that are knitted from the shoulders down to the cuffs, you need to pick up stitches from the main piece. This is simple to do, using a knitting needle and working from the right side of the work, but you need to make sure all the stitches are picked up evenly across the piece for a neat finish. For a cast-off edge, put the needle or hook into the stitches immediately below the cast-off edge. For a cast-on edge, put the needle or hook into the stitches of the cast-on row. For a row edge, put the needle or hook into the space between the edge stitch and the next stitch – but as the stitches you are picking up are wider than the rows that you are picking them up from, after every third picked-up stitch, skip one row.

One The technique is shown here along a cast-off edge, but the principle is the same on a cast-on, side edge or any other edge. With the right side of the work facing you, insert the point of a knitting needle from front to back into the knitted piece at the point you want to start picking up from. Loop the yarn around the tip of the needle.

Two Draw the loop through to the front to form a new stitch on the needle. If you start picking up on the righthand end of an edge, then the first row will be a wrong side row.

Three Continue in this way along the edge, between any markers, to pick up the number of stitches as stated in the pattern. Pull each stitch taut as you go.

EASY

Hooded Poncho

This is an easy to throw on cover-up, perfect for the beach or poolside. It is made with cotton yarn to be absorbent and breathable. Knitting cotton is different to wool as it has less elasticity, so be careful not to split the yarn when making stitches. The patch pocket is designed to be sewn on at whatever height is comfortable for you. The junior version is based on the first thing I ever made for my son Robbie and is designed for comfort. However, the fun does not have to stop once you have completed it. This garment can easily be fringed or further customised to your taste.

Measurements

Adult Size	S/M	L/XL	
Actual chest	173	213	cm
	68	83¾	in
Length	77	87	cm
	30¼	34¼	in
Hood length	38	38	cm
	15	15	in

Junior Size	One Size	
Actual chest	116	cm
	45¾	in
Length	64	cm
	25¼	in
Hood length	29	cm
	11½	in

What you will need
- Paintbox Yarns Cotton Aran 100% cotton, 85m (93 yards) per 50g (1¾ oz)

ADULT SIZE Quantity:
- **A** 18[25] x 50g (1¾ oz) balls in Sailor Blue
- **B** 4[4] x 50g (1¾ oz) balls in Grass Green

JUNIOR SIZE Quantity:
- **A** 5 x 50g (1¾ oz) balls in Marine Blue
- **B** 4 x 50g (1¾ oz) balls in Blood Orange
- **C** 1 x 50g (1¾ oz) balls in Sailor Blue
- **D** 3 x 50g (1¾ oz) balls in Buttercup Yellow
- **E** 1 x 50g (1¾ oz) ball in Pale Lilac
- **F** 2 x 50g (1¾ oz) balls in Grass Green
- **G** 1 x 50g (1¾ oz) ball in Lipstick Pink
- 1 pair 4.5mm (US 7) knitting needles
- 4.5mm (US 7) circular needle, 60cm (23 in) length
- 4mm (US 6) circular needle, 60cm (23 in) length
- Stitch holders
- Stitch marker
- Yarn needle

Tension (gauge)
18 sts and 24 rows to 10cm (4 in) over St st using 4.5mm (US 7) needles. Change needle size as necessary to achieve correct tension (gauge).

Abbreviations
See page 61.

Special techniques
Short-row shaping (see pages 90–91).

To make adult size

Back

Using 4.5mm (US 7) needles and **A**, cast on 157[193] sts and work in rib as follows:
Row 1 (RS): *P1, k1, rep from * to last st, p1.
Row 2: *K1, p1, rep from * to last st, k1.
Rep last 2 rows 5 times more, inc 1 st on last row. *158[194] sts.*
Continue in St st with rib edges as follows:
Next row (RS): Rib 9 sts as set, knit to last 9 sts, rib as set to end of row.
Next row: Rib 9 sts as set, purl to last 9 sts, rib as set to end of row.
Rep last 2 rows until work meas 77[87]cm (30¼[34¼] in) from cast-on edge, ending with RS facing for next row.

Shape shoulders

Next row: Patt to last 15[19] sts, wrap next st and turn.
Next row: Purl to last 15[19] sts, wrap next st and turn.
Next row: Knit to last 29[37] sts, wrap next st and turn.
Next row: Purl to last 29[37] sts, wrap next st and turn.
Next row: Knit to last 43[55] sts, wrap next st and turn.
Next row: Purl to last 43[55] sts, wrap next st and turn.
Next row: K14[20], turn and patt across all sts, picking up wraps as you work. Cut yarn leaving a long end.
Slip the 57[75] sts onto a holder for shoulder.
With RS of work facing, slip centre 44[44] sts onto a holder.
Rejoin yarn to rem 57[75] sts and patt across all sts, picking up wraps as you work. Cut yarn leaving a long end.
Slip the 57[75] sts onto a holder for shoulder.

Front

Work as for back until front meas 74[84]cm (29¼[33] in) from cast-on edge, ending with RS facing for next row.

Shape neck and shoulders

Next row: Patt 68[86] sts, turn and slip rem 90[108] sts onto a holder.
Next row: Cast off (bind off) 4 sts, patt to end of row. *64[82] sts.*
Next row: Patt as set to end of row.
Next row: Cast off (bind off) 3 sts, patt to end of row. *61[79] sts.*
Next row: Patt as set to end of row.
Next row: Cast off (bind off) 2 sts, patt to end of row. *59[77] sts.*
Next row: Patt as set to end of row.
Next row: Cast off (bind off) 2 sts, purl to last 15[19] sts, wrap next st and turn.
Next row: Knit.
Next row: Purl to last 29[37] sts, wrap next st and turn.
Next row: Knit.
Next row: Purl to last 43[55] sts, wrap next st and turn.
Next row: K14[20], turn and patt across all sts, picking up wraps as you work. Cut yarn leaving a long end. Slip these 57[75] sts onto a holder for shoulder.
With RS facing, slip centre 22[22] sts onto a holder.
Rejoin yarn to rem 68[86] sts and work as follows:
Next row (RS): Cast off (bind off) 4 sts, patt to end of row. *64[82] sts.*
Next row: Patt as set to end of row.
Next row: Cast off (bind off) 3 sts, patt to end of row. *61[79] sts.*
Next row: Patt as set to end of row.
Next row: Cast off (bind off) 2 sts, patt to end of row. *59[77] sts.*
Next row: Patt as set to end of row.
Next row: Cast off (bind off) 2 sts, knit to last 15[19] sts, wrap next st and turn.
Next row: Purl.
Next row: Knit to last 29[37] sts, wrap next st and turn.
Next row: Purl.
Next row: Knit to last 43[55] sts, wrap next st and turn.
Next row: P14[20], turn and patt across all sts, picking up wraps as you work. Cut yarn leaving a long end.
Slip the 57[75] sts onto a holder for shoulder.

Using **A**, join shoulders using three-needle cast off (bind off) method with wrong sides together so seams are on outside of work.

Hood

(Worked the same for both sizes.)
With RS facing, 4.5mm (US 7) circular needle and **A**, pick up and knit 18 sts down left front neck, k22 sts from front holder, pick up and knit 18 sts up right front neck, 3 sts across right back neck, k44 sts from back holder and pick up and knit 3 sts from left back neck, place marker to show start of round. *108 sts.*
Work in the round as follows:
Next round: Knit.
Change to **B** and knit 7 rounds, ending at marker. K33 sts, slip last 8 sts on to a holder, knit to end of row ending at holder. Remove marker and turn. *100 sts.*
Beg with a purl row, continue in St st until work meas 26cm (10¼ in) from pick-up edge, ending with RS facing for next row.

Shape hood top
Next row (RS dec): K47, k2tog, pm, k2, skp, knit to end. *98 sts.*
Next row: Purl.
Next row: Knit.
Next row (WS dec): Purl to 4 sts before marker, p2tog tbl, p2, sm, p2tog, purl to end. *96 sts.*
Next row: Knit.
Next row: Purl.
Next row (RS dec): Knit to 2 sts before marker, k2tog, sm, k2, skp, knit to end. *94 sts.*
Next row: Purl.
Next row: Knit.
Next row (WS dec): Purl to 4 sts before marker, p2tog tbl, p2, sm, p2tog, purl to end. *92 sts.*
Next row: Knit.
Next row: Purl.
Next row (RS dec): Knit to 2 sts before marker, k2tog, sm, k2, skp, knit to end. *90 sts.*
Next row: Purl.
Next row: Knit.
Next row (WS dec): Purl to 4 sts before marker, p2tog tbl, p2, sm, p2tog, purl to end. *88 sts.*
Next row: Knit.
Next row: Purl.
Next row (RS dec): Knit to 2 sts before marker, k2tog, sm, K2, skpo, knit to end. *86 sts.*
Next row (WS dec): Purl to 4 sts before marker, p2tog tbl, p2, sm, p2tog, purl to end. *84 sts.*
Repeat last 2 rows until 56 sts rem.
Next row: K28 sts, removing marker as you work. Slip rem 28 sts onto second needle. Fold work in half with wrong sides together so seam is on outside of work, cast off (bind off) the 2 sets of sts using three-needle cast-off (bind off) method.

Rib edging
(Worked the same for both sizes.)
With RS facing, 4mm (US 6) circular needle and **B**, starting at centre of cast-off (bound-off) stitches, pick up and knit 4 sts from centre front, 68 sts up right front to top seam, 68 sts down left front and 4 sts from centre front. Pm to show start of round. *144 sts.*
Next round: *K1, p1, rep from * to end.
Work 5 rounds in 1x1 rib, ending at marker.
Cast off (bind off) in rib.

Pocket

(Worked the same for both sizes.)
Using 4.5mm (US 7) needles and **B**, cast on 61 sts and work as follows:
Row 1 (RS): (P1, k1) 4 times, p1, knit to last 9 sts, (p1, k1) 4 times, p1.
Row 2: (K1, p1) 4 times, k1, purl to last 9 sts, (k1, p1) 4 times, k1.
Repeat last 2 rows until work meas 22cm (8¾ in) from cast-on edge.
Cast off (bind off) in patt as set.

To finish

See instructions on page 178.

To make junior size

Colour sequence for back and front

20 rows **A**	17 rows **D**
5 rows **B**	2 rows **E**
2 rows **C**	12 rows **D**
5 rows **B**	14 rows **A**
12 rows **A**	5 rows **B**
2 rows **D**	2 rows **C**
12 rows **A**	5 rows **B**
5 rows **E**	5 rows **A**
7 rows **F**	5 rows **G**
2 rows **G**	7 rows **A**
7 rows **F**	

Back

Following the colour sequence above, work as follows throughout:
Using 4.5mm (US 7) needles and **A**, cast on 107 sts.
Row 1 (RS): *P1, k1, rep from * to last st, p1.
Row 2: *K1, p1, rep from * to last st, K1.
Repeat last 2 rows 4 times more, inc 1 st on last row. *108 sts.*
Continue in St st with rib edges as follows:
Next row (RS): Rib 7 sts as set, knit to last 7 sts, rib as set to end of row.
Next row: Rib 7 sts as set, purl to last 7 sts, rib as set to end of row.
Repeat last 2 rows until work meas 61cm (24 in) from cast-on edge, ending with RS facing for next row.

Shape shoulders

Next row (RS): Patt to last 9 sts, wrap next st and turn.
Next row: Purl to last 9 sts, wrap next st and turn.
Next row: Knit to last 18 sts, wrap next st and turn.
Next row: Purl to last 18 sts, wrap next st and turn.
Next row: Knit to last 26 sts, wrap next st and turn.
Next row: Purl to last 26 sts, wrap next st and turn.
Next row: K8, turn and patt across all sts, picking up wraps as you work. Cut yarn leaving a long end.
Slip the 34 sts onto a holder for shoulder.
With RS facing, slip centre 40 sts onto a holder. Rejoin yarn to rem 34 sts and patt across all sts, picking up wraps as you work. Cut yarn leaving a long end.
Slip the 34 sts onto a holder for shoulder.

Front

Work as for back until front meas 58cm (22¾ in) from cast-on edge, ending with RS facing for next row.

Shape neck and shoulders

Next row (RS): Patt 45 sts, turn and slip rem 63 sts onto a holder.
Next row: Cast off (bind off) 4 sts, patt to end of row. *41 sts.*
Next row: Patt as set to end of row.
Next row: Cast off (bind off) 3 sts, patt to end of row. *38 sts.*
Next row: Patt as set to end of row.
Next row: Cast off (bind off) 2 sts, patt to end of row. *36 sts.*
Next row: Patt as set to end of row.
Next row: Cast off (bind off) 2 sts, purl to last 9 sts, wrap next st and turn.
Next row: Knit.
Next row: Purl to last 18 sts, wrap next st and turn.
Next row: Knit.
Next row: Purl to last 26 sts, wrap next st and turn.
Next row: K8, turn and patt across all sts, picking up wraps as you work. Cut yarn leaving a long end.
Slip the 34 sts onto a holder for shoulder.
With RS facing, slip centre 18 sts onto holder. Rejoin yarn to rem 45 sts and work as follows:
Next row (RS): Cast off (bind off) 4 sts, patt to end of row. *41 sts.*
Next row: Patt as set to end of row.
Next row: Cast off (bind off) 3 sts, patt to end of row. *38 sts.*
Next row: Patt as set to end of row.
Next row: Cast off (bind off) 2 sts, patt to

end of row. *36 sts.*
Next row: Patt as set to end of row.
Next row: Cast off (bind off) 2 sts, knit to last 9 sts, wrap next st and turn.
Next row: Purl.
Next row: Knit to last 18 sts, wrap next st and turn.
Next row: Purl.
Next row: Knit to last 26 sts, wrap next st and turn.
Next row: P8, turn and patt across all sts, picking up wraps as you work. Cut yarn leaving a long end.
Slip the 34 sts onto a holder for shoulder. Using **A**, join shoulders using three-needle cast off (bind off) method with wrong sides together so seam is on outside of work.

Colour sequence for hood

2 rows **D**	2 rows **B**
5 rows **G**	7 rows **C**
2 rows **F**	17 rows **D**
5 rows **G**	2 rows **E**
5 rows **A**	Finish hood using **D**
7 rows **C**	

Hood

Note: Pick-up and first round are worked in same colour used when finishing body. Then follow the colour sequence above.
With RS facing, 4.5mm (US 7) circular needle and **A**, starting at left shoulder seam, pick up and knit 18 sts down left front neck, 18 sts from front holder, 18 sts up right front neck, 2 sts across right back neck, 40 sts from back holder and 2 sts from left back neck, pm to show start of round. *98 sts.*
Work in the round as follows:
Next round: Knit.
Change to **D** and, following colour sequence for hood, knit 7 rounds, ending at marker. K31 sts from marker, slip last 8 sts onto a holder, knit to end of row ending at holder. Remove marker and turn. *90 sts.*
Beg with a purl row, continue in St st until work meas 16cm (6¼ in) from pick-up edge, ending with RS facing for next row.

Shape hood top
Next row (RS dec): K42, k2tog, pm, k2, skpo, knit to end of row. *88 sts.*
Next row: Purl.
Next row: Knit to 2 sts before marker, k2tog, sm, k2, skpo, knit to end of row.
Next row: Purl.
Repeat last 2 rows until 56 sts rem.
Next row: K28 sts, removing marker.
Slip rem 28 sts onto a second needle. Fold work in half and with wrong sides of work together so seam is on outside of work, cast off (bind off) the 2 sets of sts using three-needle cast off (bind off) method.

Rib edging
With RS facing, 4mm (US 6) circular needle and **B**, and starting at centre of cast-off (bound-off) sts, pick up and knit 4 sts from centre front, 54 sts up right front to top seam, 54 sts down left front and 4 sts from centre front, pm to show start of round. *116 sts.*
Next round: *K1, p1, rep from * to end.
Work 5 rounds in 1x1 rib, ending at marker.
Cast off (bind off) in rib.

Pocket
Using 4.5mm (US 7) needles and **B**, cast on 43 sts and work as follows:
Row 1 (RS): (P1, K1) 3 times, p1, knit to last 7 sts, (p1, k1) 3 times, p1.
Row 2: (K1, p1) 3 times, k1, purl to last 7 sts, (k1, p1) 3 times, k1.
Repeat last 2 rows until work meas 18cm (7 in) from cast-on edge.
Cast off (bind off) in patt as set.

To finish

Weave in any yarn ends.
For adult size, place pocket 35[40]cm (13¾[15¾] in) down from top of shoulder and 26[36]cm (10¼[14¼] in) in from each side edge to centre pocket.
For junior size, place pocket 24cm (9½ in) down from top of shoulder and 18cm (7 in) in from each side edge to centre pocket.
Pin and sew into position using duplicate stitch or whip stitch.

Knitted Homewa

res 05

Patchwork Blanket

The patches for this blanket are knitted individually then sewn together at the end. It's a fun way to practise techniques, including textured stitches, intarsia, striping, and duplicate stitch. Designed to be asymmetric with contrast colour stitching and fringing, there's no right or wrong way to make this blanket. Get together with friends to make a shared memory blanket or set yourself a goal to make a patch a week whilst taking some time out for you.

Measurements
One size
Approx. 150cm (59 in) long x 115cm (45¼ in) wide

What you will need
- Wool Couture Cheeky Chunky
  100% merino wool
  65m (71 yards) per 100g (3½ oz)
Quantity:
- **A** 5 x 100g (3½ oz) balls in Natural Cream
- **B** 3 x 100g (3½ oz) balls in Raspberry
- **C** 3 x 100g (3½ oz) balls in Aquamarine
- **D** 2 x 100g (3½ oz) balls in Aqua
- **E** 3 x 100g (3½ oz) balls in Mustard
- **F** 3 x 100g (3½ oz) balls in Baby Blue
- **G** 3 x 100g (3½ oz) balls in Lemon

- 1 pair 12mm (US 17) knitting needles
- Cable needle
- 8mm (L/11) crochet hook
- Yarn needle

Tension (gauge)
8.5 sts and 11 rows to 10cm (4 in) over St st on 12mm (US 17) needles.
Change needle size as necessary to achieve correct tension (gauge).
The tension will vary for some of the patches and is given in the instructions for these patches.

Abbreviations
See page 61.

Special techniques
Working a cable (see page 125).
Working duplicate stitch (see page 173).
Adding fringing (see pages 180–181).

Notes
This blanket has been designed as 11 separate patches. Each patch teaches a different technique.

To make

Patch one: Star stitch

Measurements
Approx. 30 x 45cm (11¾ x 17¾ in)

Yarn
A Natural Cream

Tension (gauge)
12 sts to 10cm (4 in) over pattern.

Special abbreviation
Make star: P3tog leaving sts on lefthand needle, yo, then purl 3 sts together again and allow sts to drop off lefthand needle.

Using 12mm (US 17) needles and **A**, cast on 37 sts.
Row 1 (RS): Knit.
Row 2: P1, *make star, p1, rep from * to end.
Row 3: Knit.
Row 4: P3, make star, *p1, make star, rep from * to last 3 sts, p3.
Repeat last 4 rows until work meas 45cm (17¾ in) from cast-on edge, ending with RS facing for next row.
Cast off (bind off).

Patch two: Bubble stitch

Measurements
Approx. 42 x 50cm (16½ x 19¾ in)

Yarn
B Raspberry

Tension (gauge)
8.5 sts to 10cm (4 in) over pattern.

Special abbreviation
k5B Knit 5th st below by slipping next st off lefthand needle and drop st 4 rows down, leaving 4 ladder strands across. Working from front to back, insert point of LH needle through live st on 5th row down and under strands. Using RH needle knit st normally catching ladder strands at same time.

Using 12mm (US 17) needles and **B**, cast on 35 sts.
Purl 1 row.
Work in pattern as foll:
Row 1 (RS): Knit.
Row 2: Purl.
Row 3 to 4: Rep Rows 1 to 2.
Row 5: K3, *k5B, k3, rep from * to end.
Row 6: Purl.
Row 7 to 10: Rep Rows 1 to 2 twice.
Row 11: K1, *k5B, k3, rep from * to last 2 sts, k5B, K1.
Row 12: Purl.
Repeat last 12 rows until work meas 50cm (19¾ in) from cast-on edge, ending with RS facing for next row.
Cast off (bind off).

Patch three: Intarsia check

Measurements
Approx. 42 x 45cm (16½ x 17¾ in)

Yarn
C Aquamarine
D Aqua
E Mustard

Note: Use separate balls for each square and always twist the yarn on the WS of the work when changing colour to avoid holes.

Using 12mm (US 17) needles and beg with **C**, cast on 12 sts in **C**, join **D** and cast on 12 sts in **D**, join in another ball of **C** and cast on 12 sts in **C**. *36 sts*.
Next row (RS): K12 **C**, k12 **D**, k12 **C**.
Next row: P12 **C**, p12 **D**, p12 **C**.
Repeat last 2 rows 7 times more.
Next row: K12 **D**, k12 **C**, k12 **D**.
Next row: P12 **D**, p12 **C**, p12 **D**.
Repeat last 2 rows 7 times more.
Next row: K12 **C**, k12 **D**, k12 **C**.
Next row: P12 **C**, p12 **D**, p12 **C**.
Repeat last 2 rows 7 times more.
Change to **E**.
Knit 1 row.
Purl 1 row.
Cast off (bind off).

Patch four: Wide stripe chevron in two colours

Measurements
Approx. 35 x 50cm (13¾ x 19¾ in)

Yarn
E Mustard
C Aquamarine

Tension (gauge)
9.5 sts and 10 rows to 10cm (4 in) over pattern.

Using 12mm (US 17) needles and **E**, cast on 33 sts.
Row 1 (RS): *K2tog, k2, knit into front and back of each of next 2 sts, k3, skp, rep from * to end.
Row 2: Purl.
Row 3: *K2tog, k2, knit into front and back of each of next 2 sts, k3, skp, rep from * to end.
Row 4: Purl.
Row 5: *K2tog, k2, knit into front and back of each of next 2 sts, k3, skp, rep from * to end.
Row 6: Purl.
Row 7: *K2tog, k2, knit into front and back of each of next 2 sts, k3, skp, rep from * to end.
Row 8: Purl.
Change to **C** and repeat Rows 1 to 8.
Change to **E** and repeat Rows 1 to 8.
Change to **C** and repeat Rows 1 to 8.
Change to **E** and repeat Rows 1 to 8.
Work meas 50cm (19¾ in) from cast-on edge, ending with RS facing for next row.
Cast off (bind off).

Patch five: Stocking stitch with duplicate stitch heart

Measurements
Approx. 30 x 30cm (11¾ x 11¾ in)

Yarn
A Natural Cream
D Aqua

Special abbreviations
Full stitch: Use duplicate stitch to embroider over existing knit stitch, using a V shape to cover stitch completely.
Half stitch right: Use duplicate stitch to embroider over right half of existing knit stitch, working only half of usual V shape of a duplicate stitch, working from lower left corner to upper right corner.
Half stitch left: Use duplicate stitch to embroider over left half of existing knit stitch, working only half of usual V shape of a duplicate stitch, working from lower right corner to upper left corner.

Using 12mm (US 17) needles and **A**, cast on 25 sts.
Beg with a knit row, work 32 rows in St st, ending with RS facing for next row.
Cast off (bind off).
Using **D** and working from chart, use duplicate stitch to embroider heart. Place first stitch of bottom of heart on stitch 13 of row 9 from cast-on edge.

☐ With A, knit on RS rows, purl on WS rows
■ With D, work full stitch in duplicate st
◤ With D, work half stitch right
◣ With D, work half stitch left

Patch six: Wide cable on reverse stocking stitch

Measurements
Approx. 40 x 50cm (15¾ x 19¾ in)

Yarn
F   Baby Blue

Tension (gauge)
10 sts to 10cm (4in) over pattern.

Special abbreviations
C12F (cable 12 front): slip next 6 sts onto a cable needle and hold at front of work, knit next 6 sts from LH needle, then knit sts from cable needle.
C12B (cable 12 back): slip next 6 sts onto a cable needle and hold at back of work, knit next 6 sts from LH needle, then knit sts from cable needle.

Using 12mm (US 17) needles and **F**, cast on 40 sts.
Row 1 (RS): P11, k18, p11.
Row 2: K11, p18, k11.
Row 3: P11, k6, C12F, p11.
Row 4: K11, p18, k11.
Row 5: P11, k18, p11.
Row 6: K11, p18, k11.
Row 7: P11, k18, p11.
Row 8: K11, p18, k11.
Row 9: P11, k18, p11.
Row 10: K11, p18, k11.
Row 11: P11, C12B, k6, p11.
Row 12: K11, p18, k11.
Row 13: P11, k18, p11.
Row 14: K11, p18, k11.
Row 15: P11, k18, p11.
Row 16: K11, p18, k11.
Repeat these 16 rows until work meas 50cm (19¾ in) from cast-on edge, ending with RS facing for next row.
Cast off (bind off) in pattern.

Patch seven: Moss (seed) stitch

Measurements
Approx. 30 x 30cm (11¾ x 11¾ in)

Yarn
G   Lemon

Tension (gauge)
9 sts and 12 rows to 10cm (4 in) over moss (seed) st.

Using 12mm (US 17) needles and **G**, cast on 27 sts.
Work in moss (seed) st as follows:
Next row: *K1, p1, rep from * to last st, k1.
Repeat last row until work meas 30cm (11¾ in) from cast-on edge.
Cast off (bind off) in pattern.

Patch eight: Stripe sequence

Measurements
Approx. 30 x 46.5cm (11¾ x 18¼ in)

Knitted Homewares

Yarn

- C Aquamarine
- D Aqua
- A Natural Cream
- B Raspberry
- G Lemon
- E Mustard

Using 12mm (US 17) needles and **C**, cast on 26 sts.
Beg with a knit row, work in St st as follows:

1 row **C**	8 rows **B**
2 rows **D**	5 rows **G**
3 rows **A**	3 rows **A**
5 rows **G**	2 rows **D**
8 rows **B**	1 row **C**
13 rows **E**	Cast off (bind off) using **C**.

Patch nine: Narrow stripe chevron in three colours

Measurements
Approx. 35 x 50cm (13¾ x 19¾ in)

Yarn
- G Lemon
- B Raspberry
- D Aqua

Tension (gauge)
9.5 sts and 9.5 rows to 10cm (4 in) over pattern.

Using 12mm (US 17) needles and **G**, cast on 33 sts.
Row 1 (RS): *K2tog, k2, knit into front and back of each of next 2 sts, k3, skp, rep from * to end.
Row 2: Purl.
Row 3: *K2tog, k2, knit into front and back of each of next 2 sts, k3, skp, rep from * to end.
Row 4: Purl.
Change to **B** and repeat Rows 1 to 4.
Change to **D** and repeat Rows 1 to 4.
Repeat this three-colour sequence three times more. Work should meas 50cm (19¾ in) from cast-on edge, ending with RS facing for next row.
Cast off (bind off).

Patch ten: Stocking stitch stripes with surface embroidery

Measurements
Approx. 30 x 28cm (11¾ x 11 in)

Yarn
- A Natural Cream
- E Mustard
- F Baby Blue
- B Raspberry

Using 12mm (US 17) needles and **F**, cast on 26 sts.
Beg with a knit row, work in St st as follows:

3 rows **A**	1 row **F**
1 row **E**	1 row **B**
2 rows **A**	6 rows **F**
6 rows **F**	2 rows **A**
1 row **B**	1 row **E**
1 row **F**	4 rows **A**
1 row **B**	Cast off (bind off) using **A**.

Knitted Homewares

Using the photograph as a guide, work surface crochet slip stitch to embroider 2 vertical bars of **E** and 3 vertical bars of **B**: Using a crochet hook, make a slip knot. Keep the working yarn at the back, insert hook through the fabric from front to back, yarn round hook, pull through and repeat to create each vertical lines. Fasten off.

Patch eleven: Slip stitch diamonds

Measurements
Approx. 17 x 68cm (6¾ x 26¾ in)

Yarn
A Natural Cream
G Lemon
E Mustard
D Aquamarine

Tension (gauge)
10 sts and 10 rows to 10cm (4in) over pattern.

Note: This patch is worked side to side rather than bottom up.

Using 12mm (US 17) needles and **A**, cast on 68 sts.
Row 1 (RS): Using **A**, knit.
Row 2: Using **A**, purl.
Row 3: Using **G**, k2, *sl4, k2, rep from * to end.
Row 4: Using **G**, p3, sl2, *p4, sl2, rep from * to last 3 sts, p3.
Rows 5 and 6: Using **G**, repeat Rows 1 and 2.
Row 7: Using **E**, k1, sl2, k2, *sl4, k2, rep from * to last 3 sts, sl2, k1.
Row 8: Using **E**, p1, sl1, p4, *sl2, p4, rep from * to last 2 sts, sl1, p1.
Rows 9 and 10: Using **E**, rep Rows 1 and 2.
Rows 11 and 12: Using **D**, rep Rows 3 and 4.
Rows 13 and 14: Using **D**, rep Rows 1 and 2.
Rows 15 and 16: Using **A**, rep Rows 7 and 8.
Cast off (bind off).

To finish

Using the photograph as a guide, pin the patches into position, overlapping the chevron edges at the front of the work. Sew patches together using short lengths of leftover yarn and whip stitch.

Add fringing
Cut leftover yarn into varying lengths, as follows, and leave to one side.
For top of Patch Three, cut 24 lengths of **E** approx 38cm (15 in) long.
For bottom of Patch Ten, cut 18 lengths of **C** approx 33cm (13 in) long.
For bottom of Patch Eleven, cut 14 lengths of **C** approx 70cm (27½ in) long.
For each fringe, take a length of yarn and fold in half. Push crochet hook from back to front through the raised bump of a stitch. Using the crochet hook pull the folded yarn down half-way through the stitch, then take the loop and pull the ends through to secure. Repeat along the patch edges, using the photograph as a guide. Trim each fringe to neaten, as desired.

Masterclass

Working duplicate stitch

This technique is also referred to as Swiss darning, but I call it duplicate stitch as that sums up exactly what it is – an embroidered stitch worked over the top of a finished piece to duplicate a knit stitch. Worked in the same weight yarn, the embroidered duplicate stitches will be a bit fatter and feel slightly raised. It is a fantastic way to add decoration to your knitting, like the cute heart motif here, but it's also a sneaky way to cover up any errors you didn't manage to correct while knitting.

Working duplicate stitch horizontally

One   Thread a blunt-tipped sewing needle with yarn the same weight as that used to knit with. Work from right to left. From the back, bring the needle out at the base of a knitted stitch to be embroidered. Pass the needle around the top of stitch, going under the "legs" of the stitch above.

Two   Insert the needle back through the base of the same stitch and pull the yarn taut, covering the knitted stitch completely. Bring the needle through to the base of the next stitch to the left.

Working duplicate stitch vertically

One   Work from bottom to top. From the back, bring the needle out at the base of a knitted stitch to be embroidered. Pass the needle around the top of the stitch, going under the "legs" of the stitch above.

Two   Insert the needle back through the base of the same stitch and pull the yarn taut, covering the knitted stitch completely. Bring the needle through at the base of the stitch above.

EASY

Dog Hat

I mean, who doesn't love a dog in a hat? I do love dressing up dogs; the first item I was photographed knitting at the Olympics was a jumper for Izzy the Frenchie! This fun and playful hat is knitted in neon colour stripes with contrast black, and two pompoms for added cute factor. Ideal for all pooches, from your neighbour's greyhound to your Auntie's poodle – and of course Ned, pictured here. Note of caution: a dog should never be left alone wearing any garment or with a pompom.

Measurements
One size
Head circumference 32cm (12½ in)
Finished length 22cm (8¾ in)
Will fit medium to large size dog breeds

What you will need
- Schachenmayr Bravo
  100% acrylic
  133m (145 yards) per 50g (1¾ oz)

Quantity:
- **A** 1 x 50g (1¾ oz) ball in Black (08226)
- **B** 1 x 50g (1¾ oz) ball in Neon Pink (08234)
- **C** 1 x 50g (1¾ oz) ball in Neon Green (08233)

- 1 pair 3.25mm (US 3) knitting needles
- 1 pair 3.75mm (US 5) knitting needles
- Stitch holders
- Pompom maker or cardboard for pompoms
- Scissors
- Yarn needle

Tension (gauge)
23 sts and 30 rows to 10cm (4 in) over St st on 3.75mm (US 5) needles. Change needle size as necessary to achieve correct tension (gauge).

Abbreviations
See page 61.

Special technique
Adding pompoms (see page 177).

Knitted Homewares

To make

Stripe sequence
2 rows **A**
2 rows **B**
2 rows **C**

Using 3.25mm (US 3) needles and **A**, cast on 71 sts and follow stripe sequence as given working in rib as follows:
Row 1 (RS): *K1, p1, rep from * to last st, k1.
Row 2: *P1, k1, rep from * to last st, p1.
Repeat last 2 rows a further 11 times.
Next row: Rib to last 9 sts and slip these unworked sts onto a holder. *62 sts*.
Next row: Rib to last 9 sts and slip these unworked sts onto a second holder. *53 sts*.
Change to 3.75mm (US 5) needles and starting with a knit row, continue in St st and follow stripe sequence as set until work meas 23cm (9 in) from cast-on edge, ending with RS facing for next row.

Shape crown
Row 1 (RS): K34, k2tog tbl, turn. *1 st dec*.
Row 2: Sl1, p15, p2tog, turn. *1 st dec*.
Row 3: Sl1, k15, k2tog tbl, turn. *1 st dec*.
Rep last 2 rows until 17 sts rem.
Leave rem 17 sts on stitch holder.

With RS facing, slip 9 sts from second holder onto a 3.25mm (US 3) needle, keeping stripe sequence correct pick up and knit 33 sts along side of hat, k17 sts

from crown holder, pick up and knit 33 sts along other side of hat, then rib as set across 9 sts from rem holder. *101 sts*. Starting with **A** and following stripe sequence as set, work 9 rows in rib. Cast off (bind off) using a 3.75mm (US 5) needle.

To finish

Weave in any yarn ends.
Join neckband at front.

Pompoms (make 2)
Make two pompoms (see opposite) using a pompom maker or cardboard circles approx. 6cm (2½ in) in diameter. Measure 8m (9 yards) each of 2 colours and hold together to wind the pompom. Using the long yarn ends on the pompoms, sew securely to the hat in the ear positions.

Masterclass

Adding pompoms

Who doesn't love a pompom? They bring such joy and they're a great way to use up scraps of yarn. They're really easy to make, either with a store-bought pompom maker or in the traditional way with two circles of stiff cardboard, slightly wider in diameter than the finished size of the pompom with a hole in the centre of each, measuring just under half the diameter.

One If you're using a pompom maker, open out the two parts and hold them together. Wind two yarns along each half in turn until the semicircular gap is filled, then fasten the catches. If you're using cardboard, thread a large-eyed needle with two long strands of yarn. Holding the circles together, stitch the yarn continually through the centre and around the outer edges, keeping the strands close together, until the centre space is almost filled.

Two Insert the tip of sharp scissors between the two sides of the pompom maker or two cardboard circles and snip through the layers of yarn all around the edge.

Three Slip a length of yarn through the centre space and wrap it tightly around the yarn strands. This will be the centre of the pompom. Firmly knot the yarn, leaving long ends that can later be used to attach the pompom. Remove the pompom maker or cardboard circles.

Four Fluff up the pompom and trim any uneven strands of yarn sticking out for a neat, round finish.

Stroller Blanket

EASY

A knitted blanket is a fantastic gift for a child – unique, thoughtful, and sure to become a treasured heirloom, made with love to last a lifetime. This super-simple garter stitch blanket, made using only the knit stitch, features vertical blocks of bright colours with a contrast edging and tassels along one side to show when tucked into the stroller or car seat. A machine-washable yarn is a must-have for toddlers and kids! For safety, do not add any fringing or tassels if you make this blanket for a new baby.

Measurements
One size
Approx. 60 x 90cm (23 x 35 in), excluding crochet edging and fringing

What you will need
- Hayfield Bonus Chunky
  100% acrylic
  137m (150 yards) per 100g (3½ oz)

Quantity:
- **A** 1 x 100g (3½ oz) ball in Cobalt (653)
- **B** 1 x 100g (3½ oz) ball in Emerald (916)
- **C** 1 x 100g (3½ oz) ball in Lime Green (785)
- **D** 1 x 100g (3½ oz) ball in Paprika (700)
- **E** 1 x 100g (3½ oz) ball in Raspberry (846)
- **F** 1 x 100g (3½ oz) ball in Black (965), for edging and fringing

- 1 pair 6.5mm (US 10½) knitting needles
- 6mm (US J/10) crochet hook
- Yarn needle

Tension (gauge)
13 sts and 23 rows to 10cm (4 in) over garter st on 6.5mm (US 10½) needles. Change needle size as necessary to achieve correct tension (gauge).

Abbreviations
See page 61.

Special techniques
Adding crochet edging (see page 181).
Adding fringing (see pages 180–181).

To make

Using 6.5mm (US 10½) needles and **A**, cast on 117 sts and work 30 rows garter st (knit every row).
Change to **B** and work 30 rows garter st.
Change to **C** and work 30 rows garter st.
Change to **D** and work 30 rows garter st.
Change to **E** and work 30 rows garter st.
Cast off (bind off).

To finish

Weave in any yarn ends.

Crochet edging
Using 6mm (US J/10) crochet hook, rejoin **F** to the corner of one long edge and work as follows:
Next round: Ch2 (count as 1htr), 2htr in same space, 1htr in every st to next corner, 3htr in corner, 1htr between every 2 ridges of garter st, 3htr in corner, 1htr in every st, 3htr in corner and 1htr between every 2 ridges of garter st to end of round.
Join with sl st to top of beg ch2.
Fasten off.

Fringing
Add a fringing tassel to every alternate stitch of the crochet edging along both short ends to create evenly spaced fringing that matches with each colour section of the knitted blanket.
Cut 45cm (18 in) lengths of yarn.
Hold together 2 lengths of yarn **F** and 1 length of another colour to match the knitted stitches in each section, following the photographs as a colour guide.
(In total, you will need 80 lengths of **F**, and 8 lengths each of the other 5 colours **A**, **B**, **C**, **D** and **E**.)
Fold the strands of yarn in half, so you have one folded end and one cut end.
Insert a large crochet hook through the edging stitch where you want to place the fringing tassel, from front to back.
Lay the folded end of the yarn strands over the hook.
Draw the hook back through the edging stitch, pulling the folded yarn end and strands of yarn partially through to form a loop at the front of the blanket.
Tuck the cut ends of the yarn strands through the loop and gently pull the strands to secure the tassel in place.
Repeat along the entire edge to create an evenly spaced fringing.
Trim the cut ends of the fringing to approx. 18cm (7 in), or to the length preferred, so that they are all the same length.

Masterclass

Adding a crochet edging

A crocheted border neatly finishes a knitted edge and makes a good base for fringing. Use matching yarn for a minimal subtle look, or a contrast colour for maximum impact.

One — Along the row ends of garter stitch, work a half treble crochet under the first knitted stitch on every alternate row. Bring the yarn up at one corner and work one half treble crochet into each "valley" between two rows of knit stitch.

Two — To turn the square corner, work three half treble crochets in the same place under the last edge stitch to build up a cluster of stitches.

Three — Continue along the cast-off (bound-off) edge, working one treble crochet into every stitch on the final row. Work along the cast-on edge in the same way.

Four — Draw the folded end of the tassel strands through the edging, tuck the cut ends through the loop and tighten to secure the tassel.

Caring For Your Makes

Aftercare

After pouring so much love, time and energy into creating each handknitted piece, it's essential to care for your projects. When properly looked after, they can last for many, many years and often look better with age and wear. Here is my quick guide to caring for your cherished handknits.

- **Laundering**

The most important thing when laundering an item is to follow the care instructions on the yarn label or ball band for washing or dry cleaning. I keep the yarn label in a folder or take a photo and store it on my phone. On the rare occasion a yarn label says dry clean only, remember to take the label with you to the dry cleaners, so they use the correct solvents. If something is labelled as dry clean only, you may be able to hand wash it in cold water, but always check first using a knitted tension (gauge) swatch to see what happens!

Some yarns, like acrylic or cotton, can go into the washing machine on a cold, gentle wash cycle but most animal fibres need to be hand-washed. Never wash a wool item in hot water because this will make it become 'felted', where the fabric becomes tighter and stiffer, rather than softer or more fluid. Unless this is the effect you are going for, in which case, wash away!

If your item is made up of more than one yarn, always use the gentlest method of washing. So, if you have two yarns and one says dry clean only and the other allows for machine washing, stick to dry cleaning.

Whether washing by hand or machine, always use a specially formulated wash for wool and other animal fibres or a mild detergent, which is designed for delicate fabrics. Always follow the instructions when it comes to how much wool wash or detergent to add. If something is going in the washing machine, place the detergent in the dispenser drawer rather than directly in the drum, so it does not create any unnecessary friction during the wash cycle that could damage your item.

When you are hand washing an item, use a decent-sized bowl or sink where there is space to submerge your item and for water to flow around it easily. Fill the bowl or sink with water, add the wool wash and mix this in properly before adding your item. Be gentle with it – give it a good dunk and swish the water around rather than kneading or scrubbing. If the water turns dirty quite quickly, don't be surprised. Hand-wash items are laundered less frequently than machine-wash ones, so they gather dirt and oils that swiftly leech into the water. If the water becomes murky, you can always drain it away, squeezing your item as you do so. Do not lift the item out of the sink or bowl because the weight of the water can pull it out of shape.

Nowadays, most commercially available yarns are colorfast, but it is always worth doublechecking. Take a length of yarn, wet it thoroughly and then wrap it tightly around a sheet of white paper towel. Leave the yarn to dry, then unwind it from the paper towel. If it has left behind any mark then the yarn is not colorfast.

Machine wash on cold cycle

Machine wash on gentle cycle

Hand wash in cold water

Hand wash in warm water

Do not bleach

Dry-cleanable in any solvent

Dry-cleanable in certain solvent

Do not dry-clean

Do not tumble-dry

Do not iron

Iron on a low heat

Iron on a medium heat

Caring For Your Makes

- **Removing stains**

We all have occasional accidents. In our house, spilling drinks is more of a regular occurrence. If your knitting has become stained for any reason, act swiftly, immediately blot away any excess liquid or scrape off any solid matter. Next, put some mild detergent on a clean dishcloth and directly blot the stain. Be sure to dab the fabric rather than rub it, as this can damage the fibres. Soak washable garments in cold water for 30 minutes and then rinse as if you were washing and drying normally. Stubborn stains might need to be soaked longer, like overnight.

Different stains may require different treatments – some people swear by distilled white vinegar for getting rid of alcohol and coffee stains, whilst white spirit can work wonders for oily stains.

Always be sure to check that this will not damage the yarn and can be done safely. If your garment is too delicate (or the stain is too stubborn), your local dry cleaners will be able to advise you on the best way to get the stain out or even complete the stain removal for you.

- **Rinsing and drying**

After hand washing any items, rinse them thoroughly in cold water until the water runs clear – all the soap particles that may matt the fibres or irritate sensitive skin need to be washed away. (Some specialist wool washes do not need rinsing out, so check the instructions on the bottle.) Do not wring out or twist the item to get rid of the water, instead gently squeeze out as much moisture as you can. Lift the item from the sink or basin, supporting it from underneath so that it doesn't sag, and then transfer to a clean dry towel. Roll it up in the towel to press out even more water.

Lay the item flat on a second clean, dry towel to soak up any further moisture. Reshape the item by gently patting it out before leaving it somewhere to dry. Do not use coat hangers for drying garments because your item might stretch out of shape. You need to dry your item where the air can flow around it easily but away from a direct source of heat, like a radiator, and out of direct sunlight, so avoid resting items next to windows. Instead, lie flat and ease any garments into their original shape, carefully adjusting any ribbed bands at the waist, cuffs and neckline. Fold down any collars and fasten any buttons. Lay the arms flat. You may need to dry one side and then flip it over to dry the other.

> **TOM'S TIP:**
>
> When you think about washing your sweater, ask yourself whether it could be aired instead. One of the best things about wool is that it stays fresher between washes than garments made of synthetics or cotton. Wool garments don't actually need laundering that frequently if they are well aired and rested between wears, so give them an air instead and use a liberal spritz of clothing mist spray to get rid of any odours and make them smell nice if you want. I read somewhere that "airing is caring", so follow this motto!

When drying larger items like blankets, reposition them frequently so they don't pull out of shape due to the weight of the water. Allow all items to dry for at least 24 hours, while larger items will need to be dried for at least 24 hours on each side.

If any yarn ends work themselves loose during laundering, don't be tempted to simply trim them away as this may lead to your work eventually unravelling. Pull any yarn ends all the way out and then sew them in properly again (see page XXX).

> **TOM'S TIP:**
>
> Little hole in your sweater? Don't ignore it! Always repair any holes before laundering your knitted item because the friction caused by washing can make any hole bigger. There are different ways to mend a hole, and one of my favourites is visible mending where the darning stitches are made into a decorative feature.

- ### Ironing

If your item is full of creases and needs to be ironed, proceed with caution! Always check the yarn label first and use the iron on a low setting. If the iron is too hot, this can cause discolouration and, in the worst cases, scorch markson the fabric. Avoid this by pressing down very gently on a low heat, bearing in mind that most fibres just need only a little steam to make the creases fall out.

- ### Pilling

There's nothing more annoying than those little bobbles of fluff that can appear on knitted items over time. It happens when bits of fibre separate from the strand of yarn and then become agitated, so they roll up into little balls. Pilling tends to occur in areas where there's a lot of friction, such as the sides of a sweater or around the underarms. Resist the temptation to tug at them because this can pull more of the yarn away from the strand. Instead, comb or brush them away or, after going over the item with sticky tape, use a special shaving tool to gently remove them.

Recommended Yarns

There is a yarn specified for each of the project designs in this book. You can stick with the recommended yarn. If so, you just need to pick your favourite shade. However, if you want to use a different yarn to the one specified in the pattern, you need to compare the tension (gauge) given on the yarn label (ball band) to be confident that the finished result and dimensions will not differ too dramatically from the project measurements given. The yarns used throughout this book are listed below in alphabetical order.

Cascade 220 Aran
100% Peruvian highland wool
200m (219 yards) per 100g (3½ oz)
18–20 sts to 10cm (4 in) on 4.5–5mm (US 7–8)
www.cascadeyarns.com

Coop Knits Socks Yeah!
75% fine superwash merino wool, 25% nylon
212m (232 yards) per 50g (1¾ oz)
36 sts x 50 rows to 10cm (4 in) on 2.25–2.75mm (US 1–2)
www.coopknits.co.uk

Debbie Bliss Nell
78% mohair, 13% wool, 9% polyamide
100m (109 yards) per 50g (1¾ oz)
14 sts x 20 rows to 10cm (4 in) on 6mm (US 10)
www.debbieblissonline.com

Hayfield Bonus Chunky
100% acrylic
137m (150 yards) per 100g (3½ oz)
14 sts x 19 rows to 10cm (4 in) on 6.5mm (US 10½)
www.sirdar.com

Kremke Soul Wool Karma Cotton
70% cotton, 30% recycled polyamide
105m (115 yards) per 50g (1¾ oz)
18 sts x 26 rows to 10cm (4 in) on 3–4mm (US 3–6)
www.kremkegarne.de

Paintbox Yarns Cotton Aran
100% cotton
85m (93 yards) per 50g (1¾ oz)
20 sts x 24 rows to 10cm (4 in) on 4.5mm (US 7)
www.lovecrafts.com

Rowan Big Wool
100% merino wool
80m (87 yards) per 100g (3½ oz)
7.5–9 sts x 10–12.5 rows to 10cm (4 in) on 10–16mm (US 15–19)
www.knitrowan.com

Rowan Pure Wool Superwash Worsted
100% wool
200m (219 yards) per 100g (3½ oz)
20 sts x 25 rows to 10cm (4 in) on 4.5mm (US 7)
www.knitrowan.com

Schachenmayr Bravo
100% acrylic
133m (145 yards) per 50g (1¾ oz)
22 sts x 30 rows to 10cm (4 in) on 3–4mm (US 3–6)
www.schachenmayr.com

Wool Couture Cheeky Chunky
100% merino wool
65m (71 yards) per 100g (3½ oz)
10 sts x 12 rows to 10cm (4 in) on 10mm (US 15)
www.woolcouturecompany.com

And for buttons
Textile Garden
www.textilegarden.com

Thank you ☺

I feel so lucky to be able to write a book about something that I love so much. When I first picked up a pair of knitting needles and some yarn, I could not have imagined that knitting would soon turn into one of my greatest passions.

A huge thank you to:

The team at YMU – Alex McGuire, Holly Bott, Amanda Harris, and Elise Middleton, for your continued support and help.

To the HQ team and everyone involved in creating my book, including Erika Knight and Arabella Harris at KnightKraft, Louise McKeever, Lisa Pendreigh, and Georgina Rodgers, and to the hugely talented creative team I worked with on the photoshoots, including Nikki Dupin and Emma Wells at Studio Nic&Lou. This process has been so enjoyable – thanks so much for making it a lot of fun! I am so grateful for everyone's hard work and energy in helping me realise my vision.

To Lance for introducing me to crafting (and never moaning about my growing yarn stash!) and to Robbie and Phoenix, my family and friends for appreciating my handmade gifts and cheering on my making.

To my fellow knitters – Team Great Knittin' – I can't wait to see what we make next!
#MadeWithLoveGetYourKnitsOut

HQ
An imprint of HarperCollins*Publishers* Ltd
1 London Bridge Street
London SE1 9GF

www.harpercollins.co.uk

HarperCollins*Publishers*
Macken House
39/40 Mayor Street Upper
Dublin 1
D01 C9W8
Ireland

10 9 8 7 6 5 4 3 2 1

First published in Great Britain by
HQ, an imprint of HarperCollins*Publishers* Ltd
2025

Copyright © Tom Daley 2022
Including patterns that first appeared in
Made with Love 2022

Tom Daley asserts the moral right to be
identified as the author of this work.
A catalogue record for this book is available
from the British Library.

ISBN 978-0-00-865700-0

Editorial Director: Louise McKeever
Project Editor: Lisa Pendreigh
Project Design Consultants: Erika Knight and
Arabella Harris at KnightKraft
Pattern Grading: Rosee Woodland for Light Work
Collective
Pattern Technical Editing and Proofing: Helen
Birch, Tricia Gilbert, Amelia Hodsdon, Faye
Perriam-Reed and Lynne Rowe for Light Work
Collective
Knitters and Crocheters: Judith Cheek,
Gillian Ely, Sarah Ford, Lucinda Ganderton,
Erika Knight, Sally Lee, Joanne Marsh, Lisa
Pendreigh, Karin Rayner, Jemima Schlee and
Juliana Yeo
Photography: Daniel Fraser
Photography Assistant: Andreas Parperi
Art Direction and Design: Nikki Dupin and Emma
Wells @ Studio Nic&Lou
Models: Minmie @ iMM, Naomy @ Body London,
Alanna @ Bruce and Brown and Ned the dog
Casting production: Bella Robinson
Styling: Sairey Stemp

Hair and Makeup: Liz Martins and Brady Lea
Step photography: Cara Cormack
Hand model: Chinh Hoang
Production: Halema Begum

All rights reserved. No part of this
publication may be reproduced, stored in
a retrieval system, or transmitted, in any
form or by any means, electronic, mechanical,
photocopying, recording or otherwise, without
the prior permission of the publishers.

Without limiting the author's and publisher's
exclusive rights, any unauthorized use of this
publication to train generative artificial
intelligence (AI) technologies is expressly
prohibited. HarperCollins also exercise their
rights under Article 4(3) of the Digital
Single Market Directive 2019/790 and expressly
reserve this publication from the text and
data mining exception.

Printed and bound in Malaysia by Papercraft

For more information visit:
www.harpercollins.co.uk/green